D0153173

INDIA IN TRANSITION

Freeing The Economy

INDIA IN TRANSITION

Freeing The Economy

JAGDISH BHAGWATI

CLARENDON PRESS · OXFORD

*This book has been printed digitally and produced in a standard specification
in order to ensure its continuing availability*

OXFORD
UNIVERSITY PRESS

Great Clarendon Street, Oxford OX2 6DP

Oxford University Press is a department of the University of Oxford.
It furthers the University's objective of excellence in research, scholarship,
and education by publishing worldwide in

Oxford New York

Auckland Bangkok Buenos Aires Cape Town Chennai
Dar es Salaam Delhi Hong Kong Istanbul Karachi Kolkata
Kuala Lumpur Madrid Melbourne Mexico City Mumbai Nairobi
São Paulo Shanghai Singapore Taipei Tokyo Toronto
with an associated company in Berlin

Oxford is a registered trade mark of Oxford University Press
in the UK and in certain other countries

Published in the United States
by Oxford University Press Inc., New York

© Jagdish Bhagwati 1993

The moral rights of the author have been asserted
Database right Oxford University Press (maker)

Reprinted 2002

All rights reserved. No part of this publication may be reproduced,
stored in a retrieval system, or transmitted, in any form or by any means,
without the prior permission in writing of Oxford University Press,
or as expressly permitted by law, or under terms agreed with the appropriate
reprographics rights organization. Enquiries concerning reproduction
outside the scope of the above should be sent to the Rights Department,
Oxford University Press, at the address above

You must not circulate this book in any other binding or cover
and you must impose this same condition on any acquirer

ISBN 0-19-828816-6

Jacket photographs courtesy of Sanjeer Saith

For
Abid and Karki Hussain

Preface

This volume has grown out of the three Radhakrishnan Lectures that I gave at Oxford University in the first week of June 1992. The lectures were delivered in the Ashmolean Museum, an unlikely yet apt locale for reflections on the current fortunes of a nation with an ancient civilization.

I am grateful for the hospitality extended during my stay by the Warden and Fellows of All Souls College, and for the warmth with which I was treated, at the Lectures and outside, by Sudhir Anand, Christopher Bliss, Robert Cassen, Walter Eltis, Charles Feinstein, Vijay Joshi, Sanjaya Lall, Ian Little, James Mirrlees, Tapan Raychaudhuri, Maurice Scott, Peter Sinclair, and Jonathan Vickers. I have also profited greatly from their comments and from the suggestions of many others who came to the Lectures, as also from the suggestions of T. N. Srinivasan, Paul Streeten, Richard Eckaus, Gus Ranis, Atul Kohli, and Ashutosh Varshney.

Over the years, I have learnt from the conversations and writings of many, indeed too many to acknowledge here adequately. I would be remiss however if I did not record my intellectual indebtedness to the Indian economists Pranab Bardhan, Sukhamoy Chakravarty, Padma Desai, Meghnad Desai, Suresh Tendulkar, K. Sundaram, S. Guhan, D. T. Lakdawala, P. N. Dhar, Deena Khatkhate, B. S. Minhas, Arvind Panagariya, Kirit Parikh, Isher Ahluwalia, A. M. Khusro, K. L. Krishna, Mrinal Datta Chaudhuri, Amartya Sen, Pravin Visaria, A. Vaidyanathan, K. N. Raj, Manmohan Singh, V. Dandekar, M. L. Dantwala, Deepak Lal, Sanjaya

Lall, Vijay Joshi, and, above all, to Pitambar Pant, V. K. Ramaswami, and T. N. Srinivasan.

I also recall with pleasure innumerable conversations with foreign economists who have worked over the years on, and often in, India: Ian Little, Paul Rosenstein-Rodan, Richard Eckaus, Arnold Harberger, Trevor Swan, Maurice Scott, Paul Streeten, Brian Reddaway, James Mirrlees, George Rosen, Robert Cassen, Nick Stern, and Stanislaw Wellisz. I hope that they will detect, in the tapestry that I have woven in this work, the invisible imprint of their ideas and the intellectual stimulus they gave me.

I have drawn, in this work, on some of my earlier writings, especially on the Vikram Sarabhai Memorial Lecture and the Sir Purushottam Thakurdas Memorial Lecture which I gave in the late 1980s in India, and on recent work (with Padma Desai) on the sources of friction between the United States and India in the post-war period (in Sulochana Glazer and Nathan Glazer, eds., *Conflicting Images in India and the United States*, published by the Riverdale Company of Wellesley, Mass., in 1990). But the architecture I present now is new and more substantial, and the nuances are different, changed in light of further reflection and the dramatic changes that have characterized the Indian scene since June 1991.

The economic scene today is in flux, as a result of the reforms begun in 1991, and politics remains complex and volatile. It is a hazard to end this work with a commentary on current events; new events will surely overtake some of what I say. But I hope that, regardless, the broader analysis here will remain of enduring value.

Columbia University   J.B.
New York

Table of Contents

List of Figures   x

Introduction   1

1. The Model that Couldn't   5
2. What Went Wrong?   39
3. What is to be Done?   71

Statistical Appendix   101
Index   105

List of Figures

1 A comparison of GDP per capita in India and other developing countries, 1960–88
2 Growth rates in real GNP in the Indian economy, 1952–86
3 The financing of gross domestic capital formation by gross domestic saving and foreign saving (per cent of GDP at market prices)
4 Growth rates in real GNP in the Soviet economy, 1951–80
5 Rates of literacy of people aged over 15 in selected countries in c.1990 (per cent)
6 India's export ratios relative to world exports and developing country exports, 1950–90
7 India's exports/GNP ratio, 1950–87
8 The components of gross domestic savings in India: period averages (per cent of GDP at market prices)
9 India's net public debt to GNP ratios, 1970–87
10 A comparison of consumer prices in India and other developing countries, 1950–90 (per cent change over previous year)
A1 Average life expectancy at birth in India, 1951–91
A2 The structure of GDP in India, 1980–1 prices (per cent)
A3 Employment in the organized sector in India, 1960–89
A4 The components of India's tax revenue (centre, states, and union territories), 1950/1 to 1980/1

INTRODUCTION

I find myself today in a frame of mind exactly the opposite of Bertrand Russell's when invited to speak at a dinner in honour of the American philosopher, Morris Cohen. Cohen was a man of wit. When asked by a student, 'Can you prove that I do not exist?', he is reputed to have replied, 'Maybe I can; but whom should I mail the proof to?' Sidney Hook recalls in his biography how Russell wanted to know why he should speak, was unimpressed by the reasons given, but when told that he would receive a fee of $50 for some brief remarks, promptly accepted with the observation: 'Those are fifty good reasons!'[1]

I do not have those fifty reasons to give the Radhakrishnan Lectures. I have just one, but it is compelling. Sarvapalli Radhakrishnan's distinction was unique: he held a Chair at Oxford in philosophy and the Presidency of India. Either would have sufficed to claim our attention; together, both earn our admiration. To honour him with these lectures is to honour myself.

Since Adam Smith wrote both *The Theory of Moral Sentiments* and *The Wealth of Nations*, it would not be outlandish to eulogize Radhakrishnan the philosopher by lecturing on economics. And since Radhakrishnan the President oversaw the unfolding of India's destiny in her formative years, it would not be inappropriate to turn my attention to the Indian economy.

[1] Sidney Hook, *Out of Step: An Unquiet Life in the 20th Century* (New York: Carroll & Graf Publishers, 1988 paperback edn.).

None the less, I hesitate. James Mill, in the preface to his celebrated *History of British India*, justified his effort by arguing: 'I was led to grieve, that none of those who had preceded me, in collecting for himself a knowledge of Indian affairs, had been induced to leave his collection for the benefit of others . . . if those who preceded me had neglected this important service, and in so doing were not altogether free from blame, neither should I be exempt from the same condemnation.'[2] Alas, a multitude of economists have not shied away from sharing with us their thoughts of India; indeed, little that can be said has been left unsaid. To compound my difficulty, I have myself written copiously since the early 1960s.

Returning from Oxford to India in 1962, I joined the Planning Commission and immediately found myself in the trenches of the war being waged against poverty. By the mid-1960s, when I had returned to the ivory tower to indulge my academic ambition and to seek scholarly success, I was persuaded that the framework of Indian economic policy-making was rapidly deteriorating, turning into the bureaucratic control-infested straitjacket that would stifle economic initiative and hinder development. In 1970 I (and Padma Desai) produced an intellectually coherent and sustained exposé of this sad turn of events, only to find myself turned from a progressive into a reactionary economist.[3] Years later when I returned to India, the Communist Party's official rag would denounce me as an 'average' economist; of course, if they were smart, they would have castigated me more effectively as a 'marginal' economist, with intended *double entendre*.

[2] Cf. James Mill, *The History of British India*, 5th edn., ed. Horace Wilson, (London: Piper, Stephenson and Sperice, 1858), p. xvi.
[3] Cf. J. Bhagwati and Padma Desai, *India: Planning for Industrialization* (Oxford: Oxford University Press, 1970). This was part of a pioneering project on trade and industrial policies in developing countries, at the OECD Development Center, directed by Ian Little, Tibor Scitovsky, and Maurice Scott.

But this reaction of the professional Left was complemented by that of the Left professionals, who dismissed the (Bhagwati–Desai) analysis of the failings of India's economic policies as based on 'static' analysis. So, in 1975, I (and T. N. Srinivasan) produced a further volume, demonstrating that there was no convincing way to justify these policies on the grounds that they encouraged savings, entrepreneurship, or innovation either.[4] In fact, it was somewhat odd to assert, as late as the mid-1970s, that Indian policies were conductive to rapid growth: dispassionate intellectuals were already waking up to our predicament. The gifted economist Raj Krishna would condemn India to a 'Hindu growth rate' of 3.5 per cent, an infelicitous phrasing that none the less caught popular fancy since it suggests predestination and thus captures the sense of despair that we felt about our capacity to reform and improve our performance.

I must confess to a sense of *déjà vu* as I contemplated returning to the Indian economic scene for the Radhakrishnan Lectures: kicking yet again against a stone wall is not exactly pleasurable. Imagine my surprise and exhilaration, therefore, when the new minority government of Prime Minister Rao, after the June 1991 elections, finally seized the day. Abandoning the caution and hesitation that defined the earlier efforts at liberalization, the new government has frontally embraced the philosophy of liberal economic reforms. 'Reform by storm' has supplanted the 'reform by stealth' of Mrs Gandhi's time and the 'reform with reluctance' under Rajiv Gandhi. The remarkable new Finance Minister, Manmohan Singh, with whom I share not merely St John's College in Cambridge (for the Economics Tripos) and Nuffield College in Oxford but also a common view of India's past failure and future prospects, has now

---

[4] Cf. J. Bhagwati and T. N. Srinivasan, *India*, New York: University Press, 1975. This was written as part of a substantial NBER project, directed by me and Anne Krueger, as a sequel to the OECD project noted in fn. 3.

taken India on what Jawaharlal Nehru would have called her 'tryst with destiny'.

There can then be no better time to glance back at what went wrong, to analyse why we are finally in the spring of hope, to reflect on the steps taken and the tasks ahead, and to speculate on what the future holds.

1

THE MODEL THAT COULDN'T

History has its unforeseen ironies. The post-war period, now spanning four decades through the 1980s, began with both a strong economic performance and Western empathy and approbation of India's developmental efforts and ideas. It ended with an economy in serious difficulty and, worse, the perception that India had not merely chosen the wrong economic path but had also marginalized herself in world economic affairs in consequence.

The economic realities cannot be ignored, even as India's failures must be carefully analysed, since they and their causes are more complex than commonly believed, while there are countervailing successes as well. But the perceptions of failure, disproportionate to its reality, are equally a reflection of the changing context in which India's efforts and outcomes have been placed and judged through the past forty years.

Before I turn to analysing the realities, I should therefore look at the prism through which they have been viewed, so that the distortions can be isolated and the facts separated from fiction.

PERCEPTIONS

In the 1950s India was in the hearts of both governments and economists in the West. More critically, this was so

in the United States which had emerged as the undis-
puted economic superpower at the end of the War. The
altruism and leadership of the United States would guar-
antee the reconstruction of Western Europe and Japan.
The troika of international institutions—the IMF, the
World Bank, and GATT—which she helped to construct
as the War ended would provide the infrastructure that
smoothed the transition of the war-torn economies to
the golden age of the 1950s and 1960s. Her bilateral aid
programme, soon to reach out to several developing
countries, would be a barometer of her readiness to play
the leading role in the challenge of development.

The new Soviet threat to security and the growing
Cold War reinforced, even overwhelmed, altruism in
these matters with enlightened self-interest. The support
for India, and the perception of her success, would then
vary with the ebb and flow of the Cold War and with
the dramatic shifts in the relations between the two communist giants, China and the Soviet Union. Four turns
of the kaleidoscope can be distinguished.

The Early Years

The early years, through to the mid-1960s, witnessed an
optimistic assessment of India's potential and performance because, despite the irritant of Prime Minister
Nehru's non-alignment and his steadfast advocacy of
mainland China's cause in the teeth of US unwillingness
even to admit China into the United Nations, India's
economy was widely considered by mainstream
American intellectuals and élite to be a democratic
experiment in development and hence perceived as an
alternative to China's totalitarian path. If China suc-
ceeded and India did not, the totalitarian model,
embraced by the Soviet Union and her ally China,
would exercise a profound impact on the leadership of
the developing countries, pushing them ever more cer-

tainly into the Soviet orbit of influence. The early writings of Walt Rostow, Max Milliken, Paul Rosenstein-Rodan, and the many other economists such as Wilfred Malenbaum, George Rosen, and the Oxbridge dons Ian Little and Brian Reddaway, who came to India on the programmes sponsored by the MIT Center for International Studies and the Ford Foundation during the 1950s and until the mid-1960s, were thus extremely optimistic and well-disposed towards Indian planning efforts and methods. A favourable contrast with China was uppermost in their minds and often explicit in their writings, especially those of Malenbaum and Rostow.[1]

Many of these were also among the major advisers, from across the Charles River in Cambridge, Massachusetts, to Senator John Kennedy on foreign aid programmes and were his theoreticians on the effectiveness of aid in defeating the Soviet Union in the Cold War in the Third World. They tended to see much good in India's efforts, certainly more and for longer than many others not so committed to democracy's virtues. President Kennedy and his Ambassador, John Kenneth Galbraith, fully carried this tradition forward. When the border war erupted between China and India in 1962, President Kennedy's sympathy and aid for India were immediate, and indeed a far cry from the reverse anti-Indian policy bias that President Nixon would demonstrate a decade later.

That China's economic success would be considered a nightmare was understandable. Unlike Eastern Europe, which had fallen to communism from virtual conquest, China's communist regime was the product of indigenous revolution. Her military might, her sheer size, and the

---

[1] It is manifest also in the later, highly successful work of J. Lewis, *Quiet Crisis in India* (Washington, DC: The Brookings Institution, 1962), where the author offers an optimistic assessment of India's developmental strategy and prospects and makes an eloquent appeal for aid and other support.

widespread assumption that the huge population would now be successfully harnessed to great economic tasks, conjured up the vision of a slumbering giant, finally awake, certain to fill the landscape with his presence. Indeed, China was no Cuba.

The choice of India as the counterfoil to China reflected some parallel, and other contrasting, factors. Her size was also immense, if not equal to China's. But her independence had resulted from the politics of peace and her chosen ways were those of Western democracies. She was thus the world's most populous democracy, a substantial and fitting candidate for the contest with China.

But she was also an excellent horse to put your bets on. Her leadership was world class: Mahatma Gandhi and Jawaharlal Nehru were names to conjure with, and Nehru would indeed provide continuity and stability through India's early decades. The Congress Party did as well: seasoned by long struggle, dominant on the political landscape, it appeared to provide an anchor to the new democracy that might otherwise be overwhelmed by political fragmentation. The civil service, the mandarin system left behind by the British, was renowned for high competence and incorruptibility. As you looked across the Third World, it was indeed hard to find a country that offered more if you were judging development potential.

Sheer altruism would also have supported the choice of India as the favoured target of attention and aspiration. The immense poverty and the numbers of the poor were staggering. If the task this set for India was daunting, and might have led to despair, it also defined an agenda and the passion with which it would be pursued. Contrary to what it has now become fashionable to assert, and I shall argue this later, the removal of this poverty was the central goal of the developmental effort that India undertook; the means included principally the creation of more income and wealth, through growth, with a view to pulling up the impoverished into gainful employment.

Thus, India's economic development, for a constellation of reasons, drew support in the 1950s through to the mid-1960s. This was reflected in the influx of economists from around the world to share in the task and in the rewards of success. Honey attracts flies; gold attracts diggers; and India attracted economists. I mentioned earlier those who came under US programmes. But many more came in other ways. They were particularly evident when Professor Mahalanobis began work on the Second Five-Year Plan that would shift emphasis to building India's heavy industry and begin equally the slide into India's bureaucratic ways and her inward-looking, relatively autarkic policies. They included the first two Nobel Laureates in Economics: Ragnar Frisch of Norway and Jan Tinbergen of the Netherlands.

An audience with Prime Minister Nehru was a principal dividend promised to all visitors of distinction. Nehru enjoyed intellectual discourse, but talking to economists was something else. Pitambar Pant, the great Indian planner with whom I worked when I returned from Oxford in 1962, told me about the time Ragnar Frisch was taken to tea with Nehru. An austere man, whose planning approach required that a social objective function (defining the trade-offs among different desired targets such as income and employment) be maximized subject to resource and technological constraints to derive an optimal developmental plan, Frisch had been frustrated by the lack of input into such an objective function. Now that he had Nehru captive, he cross-examined him mercilessly: how much employment would he give up today to get more employment tomorrow; how much employment would he trade for income now; and so on and on. When the tea had mercifully ended and Frisch had been escorted out, Nehru called Pant back and quietly told him: 'Never bring that man back to me again'.

India thus enjoyed until the late 1960s the indulgence that would minimize the warts in her policies, exaggerate her performance and her potential, and also produce aid support. Here, I must remind you that, in the economic race set between India and China, between democracy and totalitarianism, the economists certainly felt that India faced a handicap that only aid could offset. The (Harrod–Domar) model of economic analysis that was used to think about development was essentially focused on two parameters: the rate of investment and the productivity of capital. But, for policy purposes, the latter was largely treated as 'given' and the policy question was therefore centred on the raising of the rate of investment.[2] This mainstream economist's approach coincided with the Marxist focus on 'primitive accumulation' as the mainspring of industrialization and also with the quasi-Marxist models of the investment-allocation literature that grew up around Maurice Dobb.

But if the focus was on accumulation, with its productivity considered as a datum, it was evident that democracies would be at a disadvantage relative to totalitarian countries. Totalitarian countries could extract savings that democracies could not. Thus, writing in the mid-1960s, I noted 'the cruel choice between rapid (self-sustained) expansion and democratic processes'.[3] The Princeton political scientist Atul Kohli has christened this the 'cruel choice' thesis.[4] It was widely shared by economists at the time, though later, as I argue below, the thinking would shift away from raising the rate of

---

[2] I return to this distinction at length later in Ch. 2.

[3] Cf. J. Bhagwati, *The Economics of Underdeveloped Countries* (London: Weidenfeld and Nicholson; New York: McGraw-Hill, 1966), 204.

[4] Cf. A. Kohli, 'Democracy and Development' in J. P. Lewis and V. Kallab (eds.), *Development Strategies Reconsidered* (Washington, DC: Overseas Development Council, 1986), 156. Also see the discussion in J. Bhagwati, 'Democracy and Development', *Journal of Democracy*, 3(3) (July 1992), 37–44.

savings and investment (a dimension on which most developing countries, including India, did well) to getting the most out of one's blood, sweat, and tears (a dimension on which the developing countries performed in diverse ways and India failed). Indeed, by the 1970s, it was manifest that the policy framework defining the productivity of investment was absolutely critical, and the winners and losers would be sorted out by the choices they made in this regard. And democracy no longer looked that bad after all: it could provide better incentives, relate development to people, and offset any accumulationist disadvantage that it could produce. But, at the time, the 'cruel choice' thesis implied immediately that India was handicapped in the race with China. Therefore, India's democratic experiment not merely deserved help; it needed it as well.[5]

Changing Alliances

This conjunction of factors favouring both aid for India and a sympathetic view of her potential and performance worked, of course, in the contrary direction for China. It was also to be rudely interrupted by the constellation of events that brought the United States closer to China and led India closer instead to the Soviet Union.

Starting with the US overture to Beijing, and the 1972 Nixon–Chou summit's 'Shanghai Communiqué' calling for the development of trade and cultural ties, 'normalization' of Sino–US relations moved into high gear. The potential for such moves had been evident since the Sino–Soviet split; Nixon's genius lay in translating that potential into foreign policy.

At the same time, as a result of the infamous Nixon–Kissinger tilt towards Pakistan and against India

---

[5] I return to the effect of India's democracy on her economic performance later.

during the 1971 war over East Pakistan's demand for the creation of Bangladesh and by the potential Chinese threat from the northern border, India was catapulted into the Treaty of Peace, Friendship and Co-operation with the Soviet Union of 9 August 1971. Mrs Gandhi's September visit to Moscow, and Soviet President Podgorny's October visit to New Delhi quickly followed, and the Soviet Union obliged by twice vetoing calls by the Security Council for an immediate ceasefire in the Indo-Pakistan War as the Indian army was winning the war and Bangladesh was being born.

This would usher in an era where the Chinese economy would now be viewed with indulgence whereas India's was perceived critically. Two factors seem to have further accentuated this reversal in Indian and Chinese image-distortion in US eyes.

First, the American Sinologists seem to have worn blinkers during the 1970s, overcompensating perhaps for the earlier years of anti-Chinese ethos in the United States, though a few nonconformist Sinologists such as Lucien Pye and Edward Friedman seem to have been more cautious than the rest. Thus, for instance, Neville Maxwell and Bruce McFarlane reported in their Editors' Introduction to the special issue of *World Development* on 'China's Changed Road to Development' (1983, pp. 627–8), based on a September 1982 Oxford Conference, that:

A challenge was issued by Friedman that we should discount most of the facts provided by Chinese sources and start again. This was preferable, he thought, to falling back on meaningless abstract theorizing about what might be happening in China. Friedman quoted as examples of the extreme dangers of 'Sinology', the very late discovery by Westerners of 15 million deaths in China after the 1959–61 attempt to get a higher surplus out of agriculture and the long delay on the part of Western socialists in unmasking the terrible dangers of a self-reliance model gone mad, such as the Cultural Revolution at its peak and Pol Pot's strategy for Cambodia, which was a variant of it.

But these were dissident views.

Second, in a reversal of the ideological preferences of the intellectuals' rank-ordering of India and China during the 1960s, the mid-1970s saw a new generation of comparative analysts in the United States: the radical and quasi-radical economists. Freshly returned from a China which was now opening to view but still not beginning to change gear to become a gung-ho 'capitalist roader', these economists rooted for the radical China rather than for the capitalist India. Among the more notable examples of this turnabout occurred at the San Francisco meeting of the American Economic Association in December 1974, where a panel on 'China and India: Development During the Last 25 Years' featured Thomas Weisskopf and Barry Richman, both of whom found China to be Pareto-better (i.e. better on every dimension) than India.[6]

However, as the 1970s wore on, and the Chinese themselves began to lament the excesses of the Cultural Revolution, and it became evident that there was a wide disparity between assertions and realities in regard to both growth and poverty,[7] and the new Chinese leadership began to shift course on economic ideology by 1978, the radical fascination with China began to disintegrate. In any event, the rise of conservatism in the United States by the end of the decade had already emasculated the potency of the radical views as influential commentary.

---

[6] See P. Desai's riposte, combining mild ridicule with economic analysis: 'China and India: Development During the Last 25 Years', *American Economic Review*, 65(2) (1975).

[7] The quote on Friedman, above, illustrates this well.

Market Reforms

Indeed, the pronounced shift in Chinese economic strategy towards economic reforms that began in 1978 and reached full throttle by the early 1980s, greatly reinforced the predisposition to a favourable view of China's economic performance that the Sino–Soviet split, and their mutual hostility, had produced. Combined with the resurgence of conservative intellectual and economic thinking in the United States, this shift in China's external politics and internal economics produced, in yet another turn of the kaleidoscope, a highly romanticized view of China's economic performance and potential.[8]

But India too benefited belatedly from a similar shift of perceptions, though on a more limited scale. Rajiv Gandhi assumed office as Prime Minister in 1984, following Mrs Gandhi's assassination, and brought a fresh promise of market-oriented economic reforms, reaping the same harvest of goodwill that China's more drastic shift of gear (from the confines of communist ideology) was yielding in greater abundance for Premier Deng Xiaoping. Again, the perceptions were running ahead of the realities.

And the perceptions were driven now, not by whether economic performance was remarkable, but by whether the policy framework was changing in the direction of market-oriented reforms. India's continued profession of friendship with the Soviet Union remained an irritant; but it did not compromise the changing perception of India's economic prospects.

Again, a contributing cause was the World Bank's influential, optimistic assessments of both countries. One cannot altogether dismiss the thought that, plagued by debt-ridden Latin American clients, collapsing African economies, and opposition by the first Reagan

---

[8] Cf. the interesting columns on China in the *New York Times* by L. Silk after his visit there; especially on 27 Oct. 1985, on 'China Hits Its Stride'.

Administration to IDA replenishments and Extended Fund Facility loans, the Bank was eager to find successes.

I should add that the enthusiastic foreign assessments reflected partly the domestic prevalence of high expectations in both countries. In particular, the Chinese (while optimism in regard to the acceleration of growth was certainly justified) seemed to have gone overboard, if the reports that came through from visitors and their own occasional pronouncements are an accurate guide, in expecting economic miracles from their new policies. Indeed, the changes that the Chinese authorities made in the late 1970s and early 1980s were accompanied by astonishing Chinese claims as to their anticipated growth rates, 11 per cent being cited for the early years and an acceleration even to 18 per cent. Now, anything is possible for very short periods—imagine going from a bad drought suddenly to an abundant harvest in China, or a war-devastated agriculture being restored merely to its normal trend line. But development economists with any historical sense must find it implausible to entertain such claims with a straight face. Indeed, with 80 per cent of its labour-force in agriculture, where long-sustained growth rates of even 4 per cent are considered a supreme achievement, you would need a Confucian miracle for such manna to fall from the capitalist skies. It would appear as if the Chinese leaders had moved from one Great Leap Forward to another: Chairman Mao's was to be taken by Marx's altruistic, complete man; Mr Deng's was to be taken by Adam Smith's selfish, economic man.

By contrast, Indian expectations, while aroused, were somewhat modest. It is fair to say that the euphoria exhibited in the United States[9] was not shared in the

[9] The *Wall Street Journal*, in particular, mistakenly saw a Reagan in Rajiv Gandhi and applauded India's turn from defunct socialist doctrines. The applause turned out to be premature. In any event, the analogy was

same degree by Indians, much as they supported their young Prime Minister's declarations and initiatives supportive of 'liberal,' market-oriented economic reform. There is nothing in Indian pronouncements of this period which compares with the unrestrained optimism and expectations of the Chinese leadership. Yet many in India did feel that finally India had turned the corner and an 'economic miracle' might well be at hand if only the Prime Minister could stay the course. In the event, he did not.

China's Fall from Favour

But the final turn of the kaleidoscope came, returning China to disfavour and India to some indulgence, as the 1980s ended.

The collapse of the Soviet Union and her empire took away the main irritant between the United States and India and the main (security) reason for regarding China as a valuable counterweight to Soviet power. After Rajiv Gandhi's defeat at the polls in 1989, the two successive minority non-Congress governments that followed, and Rajiv Gandhi's assassination, Prime Minister Narasimha Rao took office with a minority Congress government. Facing a serious macroeconomic and foreign-exchange crisis, he and his Finance Minister, Dr Manmohan Singh, unleashed dramatic economic reforms.

But if India was moving in the right direction in internal economic reform, China had moved in the wrong direction in internal political reform. The Tiananmen Square Massacre of June 1989 set the Chinese image back to what it had been during the period of the worst excesses of the Red Guards under Chairman Mao and the Gang of Four. It also put into power the hard-liners

misleading. Rajiv Gandhi disapproved of mindless controls but was keen to have an active government role in areas such as education. His reforms were aimed at changing the nature of intervention, not at emasculating it.

opposed to the economic reforms of the 1980s. In the Western rank-ordering of the two countries, and the attitudes that would shape the perceptions of their economic performance and prospects, we had come a full circle, ending almost where we started in the 1950s.

But not quite. Where the West had earlier regarded the two Asian giants as the sure bets in the developmental race, the only question being the order in which they would finish, the race had ended with altogether different dark horses at the finish line. The success stories turned out to be the smaller countries of the Far East, their developmental strategies becoming the focus of universal attention. Both India and China had fallen behind, trying to catch up in the 1980s, with reforms whose inspiration came partly from the successes of these others.

In particular, India's model of development had turned out to be the one that couldn't. What it was and why it couldn't will be the subject of my analysis in the next chapter. For the present, however, let me simply draw the main contours of India's disappointing performance.

REALITY

The disappointment with Indian economic performance lies in her lack-lustre growth for a quarter of a century. It lies equally in her consequent inability to remove a significant part of the poverty that afflicts her population.

Then again, the framework of her economic policies (as defined by the iron fist of controls over the private sector, the spreading stain of inefficient public enterprises, and an inward-looking trade and investment strategy)[10] has produced, not merely the dismal

---

[10] I focus on these, to the exclusion of India's successful policies and performance, for example, in transforming traditional agriculture, and the

economic performance, but also the added sense of a senseless adherence to policies that have long been seen by others to have little rationale. The disenchantment with India's 'model' of development has therefore come from both her inadequate performance and from the widely-shared and justified perception that her policies have been wittingly foolish. In fact, since judgements are formed by most of us only from the immediacy of our experience, encounters with these irrational policies[11] have produced greater disenchantment than their deleterious consequences for growth and poverty which are understood only by a limited few. After all, if you see anyone furiously feasting on fatty foods as his daily diet, you are likely to doubt his sanity even if his measured cholesterol levels are not within your reach.

Political Success

However, any objective analysis of India's economic performance must be placed at the outset in the context of her political triumph: her democracy and the management and maintenance of stability despite the fissiparous nature of multi-ethnicity and of the zero-sum politics of acute scarcity. With today's worldwide instability in multi-ethnic nations, it is easier to appreciate the skills with which India managed to contain the issue, even as the Kashmir and the Punjab problems have now reached crisis point. Writing in 1960, the noted American journalist Selig Harrison recorded his forebodings in his celebrated work, *India: The Most Dangerous Decades*,[12] citing in particular the anti-Hindi sentiment in the south

improvement in the average life expectancy at birth (Fig. A1 in the Statistical Appendix). The analysis of this inefficient framework is the subject of Ch. 2.

[11] For instance, there was endless interference with production and investment decisions, extending to whether you would continue producing plastic toys or shift to buckets, and penalties for improving capacity output beyond that officially sanctioned.

[12] Princeton, NJ: Princeton University Press.

that would soon fuel separatist demands and the agitation for reorganization of state boundaries by language as elemental forces that could splinter the nation. But these came to nought. As one of my witty friends from Tamil Nadu put it later to Harrison: 'We tried to implement your agenda, but you know how inefficient we are.'[13] By contrast, Pakistan proceeded relentlessly to bifurcation, Nigeria turned to bitter civil war, and much of Africa was reduced to inter-tribal warfare.

The greater triumph was India's democratic politics (which, of course, cannot be separated altogether from India's ability to contain the fissiparous forces). As the world has turned almost universally to democracy, it is hard to recollect that India stood almost alone in Asia, Africa, and Latin America in her strong commitment to the democratic institutions of free elections, an independent judiciary, and a lively press.

Mrs Gandhi's brief suspension of fundamental rights during her ill-advised Emergency only showed in the end the strength of the democracy that had taken root. Turning to elections, Mrs Gandhi lost power and accepted the new government in a peaceful transition, belying the fear that the vast, illiterate population would not care about democracy and that only the educated élite worried about *habeas corpus*, elections, etc. My favourite witticism during the Emergency was that when Mrs Gandhi returned to the electorate, she would give up universal suffrage for a literacy test as once in the United States, but with a difference: only those who failed the test would be allowed to vote. But the reality turned out to be more comforting.

The poor and the illiterate seem to value their democratic rights equally, if not with greater passion. If one thought of them as a mindless, lumpen-proletariat and peasantry, or if one worked from Barrington Moore's

---

[13] Cited in P. Desai, fn. 6, above.

classic and persuasive thesis[14] that it was the rise of the bourgeoisie that had historically ushered in democracy, or if one looked at the sorry spectacle of the undemocratic politics in most of the new countries, this was indeed a revelation. But it is not difficult to understand. A functioning democracy provides the poor with the power to assert themselves, even as their economic situation and social circumstance reduce them to impotence. It is unlikely that, offered the choice between the continuation of democracy and its demise, they would hesitate. And they did not in India. The culture of democracy turned out to be self-reinforcing.

But can it be argued that India's disappointing economic outcome was a result of a trade-off between her political preference for democracy and her economic performance? I do not think so. India's political virtue must be applauded for itself; it cannot be invoked to justify her (relative) economic failings.[15] This contention may be justified in several ways:

• There is no simple relationship between democracy and growth rates if cross-country regressions are run.

• Again, for any successful countries (e.g. South Korea and Singapore) which have been authoritarian, there are others with lack-lustre performance and no democracy either (e.g. Zaïre, the Soviet Union, and Argentina earlier). Authoritarianism seems to be neither a necessary

---

[14] Cf. B. Moore, *Social Origins of Dictatorship and Democracy* (Boston, Mass: Beacon Press, 1966). See also R. Dahrendorf, *Society and Democracy in Germany*, (New York: Doubleday, 1969), and Bhagwati, fn. 4, above.

[15] In his forthcoming book, *Democracy, Development and the Countryside: Urban–Rural Struggles in India*, Cambridge: Cambridge University Press (New York and Cambridge: 1993), and in other articles (e.g., 'India's Democratic Exceptionalism and its Troubled Trajectory', mimeo, Harvard University, Department of Government), the political scientist A. Varshney has explored this question more broadly and in greater depth. He concludes that, despite her democracy, India could have adopted a better policy framework that would have yielded a significant improvement in her economic performance, even though not as substantial as South Korea's.

nor a sufficient condition for rapid growth, on such evidence.[16]

• The rapid growth of the Far Eastern countries, usually considered to be a result of their authoritarian politics, seems to me to be attributable instead to their geographical and intellectual proximity to Japan. Their outward orientation in trade (which enabled them to profit greatly from the rapid expansion of world trade in the 1950s and 1960s and positioned them to compete successfully in the less prosperous 1970s and 1980s) and their total commitment to literacy and education (which are critical 'fundamentals' in growth), were both major components of Japan's strategy of rapid growth. By contrast, India drew her policy ideas from Fabian politics and English economics, neither of which served her economy well. To attribute the Far Eastern nations' success to their authoritarian politics and India's (relative) failure to her democratic politics is simply a *non sequitur*, a classic example of the *post hoc ergo propter hoc* fallacy, in my judgement.

• I would also remind you that the fear that India would not be able raise her savings rate, due to democratic politics curtailing the capacity to tax, turned out to be unfounded for two reasons. The post-war experience showed that savings did increase considerably. Moreover, the increased savings primarily came from the private sector,[17] so that the need for fiscal policy to be the prime instrument for raising the nation's savings rate turned out to be far less critical. (Note also the facts that the failure of the public-sector enterprises (which is by no means confined to the democratic countries but is a fairly universal phenomenon) reduced the rise in the national savings rate by producing, in many cases, losses rather than profits, and that the substantial rise in tax revenue as a proportion of GDP, to 17.2 per cent in

---

[16] Kohli, fn. 4, above, Table 1, p. 157.   [17] See Fig. 8, in Ch. 2, below.

1989/90, was offset by an explosion of subsidies and
other current expenditures and transfers.)[18]

Growth

India's failings are manifest in her slow rates of growth
of income and per capita income. India had set herself
the task of doubling her income, starting from the First
Five-Year Plan in 1950, by 1967/8, with per capita
income doubling by 1973/4. The rise in national income
during 1951–6 having been above projected levels, the
planners even expected an improvement over these targets.[19] Defining the need for a 'step-up in investment in
the second and third plan periods', the authors of the
Second Plan noted that 'These ten years may, therefore,
be regarded as the most crucial in determining the further course of development.'[20] In fact, the projected
increases in per capita income showed that the entire
fifteen-year period until the end of the Fourth Plan was
characterized by optimistic expectations, reflecting growing investment rates offset only partially by a rise in the
marginal capital-output ratio (reflecting partly the investment shift to heavy industry in the Second Plan).

Instead, this period turned out, extending through to
the end of the 1970s, to be a disappointment. Not
merely did India's weak performance in increasing
income and per capita income fall below her own aspirations. It also put India behind many developing countries in this race, and way behind the super-performers
of the Far East.

Fig. 1 underlines this forcefully. Using data based on
the Heston–Summers purchasing-power parity calculations

[18] In the 1980s, the public sector became the conduit for macroeconomic
disequilibrium and the crisis then precipitated the current reforms, as discussed in Ch. 2.
[19] Cf. *The Second Five-Year Plan* (New Delhi: Government of India,
Planning Commission, 1956), 9–11.
[20] Ibid. 11.

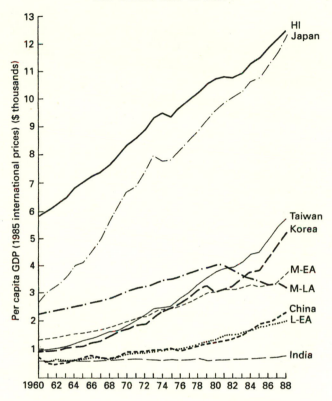

Fig. 1. A comparison of GDP per capita in India and other develop-
ing countries, 1960–88
Key:
HI High-income countries
M-EA Middle-income countries in East Asia
M-LA Middle-income countries in Latin America
L-EA Low-income countries in East Asia
Source: The World Bank.

at 1985 prices for 21 'high income' and 88 developing
countries since 1960, this chart shows up India's sorry
performance.[21] She performs appallingly through 1980
compared to the super-performers Taiwan, South Korea,

[21] The Indian curve looks flatter than it should for the 1980s, due to scale,
but the relative performances are manifest.

and Japan, but she also loses out, if not so dramatically, to the average performance of both middle-income and low-income East Asia. The Latin American performance is also better. But in the 1970s, it is ephemeral, based on debt-led growth that would go into reverse gear during the 1980s when India did better instead.

Of course India's comparatively low growth rate must be judged with care. It has been defended in various ways, outlined below, but without carrying conviction.

• Growth now may be at the expense of growth later, as illustrated by the Latin American contrast during the 1970s and the 1980s. Also, we know that a growth strategy may be optimally characterized by a J-curve: putty-clay models can readily lead to such strategies. But this sophistication has no relevance to judging India's weak performance.

• Then again, it is commonly argued in India that, compared to the pre-independence period under British rule, the Indian growth rate has been remarkable.[22] Indeed it has. But a similar, and more striking contrast obtains for the countries with superior performance. No comfort can be drawn in this fashion if you must defend the Indian record.

• Then there is the perennial excuse: the success of others is special and cannot be used to judge India which is 'different'. A typical argument is that the Far Eastern economies were 'small' and therefore could grow at high rates that could apply to small parts of India but not be extended over all of India.[23] Would we argue equally

---

[22] Cf. S. Chakravarty, *Development Planning: The Indian Experience*, 1985 Radhakrishan Lectures (Oxford: Oxford University Press, 1987). For earlier observations on the acceleration in the post-1947 growth rate in India, see also M. Milliken, 'India in Transition: Economic Development: Performance and Prospects', *Foreign Affairs*, 46(3) (April 1968), 532–47, and K. N. Raj, *Indian Economic Growth: Performance and Prospects* (Delhi: Allied Publishers, 1965), among several studies.

[23] Cf. A. Ghosh, 'Indian Development Strategy: An Exchange of Views', *Economic and Political Weekly* 26(29) (25 September 1991), 2234–6.

then that, since other small (even smaller) countries have not grown much, India's larger size is an advantage and her growth rate should have been higher? In fact, if one wants a theoretical analysis of size (in terms of income) and its impact on growth, the most likely candidate is one that would favour India, not handicap it: increasing returns would be exploited perhaps more fully in countries of larger size (unless international markets were reasonably free) and, *ceteris paribus*, lead to higher growth as well.[24] In any event, there are perfectly good, universal reasons from economic analysis that can explain India's weak performance, as I shall discuss later.

Poverty

But one final irony of the disappointing growth rate has been that it has seriously handicapped the alleviation of poverty in India. The principal problem in India is manifestly her poverty. With 14 per cent of the world's population, India has the misfortune of having almost twice as large a share of the world's poor. Recent estimates of poverty in India, and this is a growth industry among economic statisticians there, suggest that the percentage of those considered poor exceeded a quarter of India's population even at the end of the 1980s.[25]

When I argue that India's disappointing growth had a major role in her disappointing performance in the war against poverty, I must remind you that this thoroughly plausible statement can create immense controversy in India. The adverse reaction comes mainly from three

[24] The recent growth-theoretic models of Lucas and Roemer have also provided the analytical basis for the assertion that increasing returns may lead to higher steady-state growth.

[25] For a recent discussion, see M. Ravallion and K. Subbarao, 'Adjustment and Human Development in India' (Washington DC: World Bank, mimeo, March 1992). The estimates used by these authors are the 'head-count' measure of poverty. But other measures tell a similar story. See also the important contributions by B. S. Minhas, S. Tendulkar, and others, noted later in this chapter.

'anti-growth' fallacies that are deep-seated in ideological thinking, though there is a residual area of genuine difference of judgement.

Fallacy 1: *The removal of poverty requires 'direct' anti-poverty programmes, not growth.* The assertion of the irrelevance of growth to the anti-poverty objective is simply wrong. With the amelioration of poverty as the target, the policy instruments designed to achieve that target can be divided into two main classes: (i) the indirect route, i.e. the use of resources to accelerate growth and thereby impact on the incomes and hence the living standards of the poor; and (ii) the direct route, i.e. the public provision of minimum-needs-oriented education, housing, nutritional supplements, and health, and transfers to finance private expenditures on these and other components of the living standards of the poor.

The primary distinction between the two approaches is between creating income (and hence consumption) and providing consumption (in kind or through doles).[26] The latter necessarily involves redistribution between different groups unless the financing comes from external resources; the former need have no such component, though complementary policies to bias the creation of income towards the poor will often involve redistributive elements. Indeed, within both approaches, the direct and the indirect, we can consider the question of 'biasing' or 'targeting' the policies in favour of the poor. Thus, the indirect growth-oriented route may be supplemented by policies facilitating borrowing and investment by the poor or by redistributive land reform, whereas the direct route may be explicitly targeted towards the poor via

---

[26] Of course, the latter in turn can have productivity effects that improve incomes and also growth perhaps. In that case, one can eat one's cake and have it too. But, at some stage, the tradeoff will take over. For further analysis of the relationship between the two approaches, see my Vikram Sarabhai Memorial Lecture, 'Poverty and Public Policy', *World Development*, 16(5) (1988), 539–55.

means tests or choice of health and nutritional programmes that overwhelmingly benefit the poor.

The optimal policy design should generally involve a
mix of these two approaches unless the 'productivity' of
either in achieving the target overwhelmingly dominates
that of the other. Thus, for instance, if growth will concentrate increased incomes entirely among the non-poor
and there is no upward mobility either, the relevant rate
of return to the indirect route is zero. Indeed, if growth
can be shown to be immiserizing to the poor, this return
would be negative. In this event, the case for exclusive
reliance on the direct route appears overwhelming.

But, even then, the case is crippled by two compelling
provisos. First, it should be shown that the factors, both
economic and political, that constrain the effectiveness of
the growth process in indirectly reducing poverty do not
simultaneously and equally afflict the direct route and
prevent it too from effectively providing benefits to the
poor. And second, the neglect of the growth process,
even if its indirect impact on poverty through increased
incomes for the poor is negligible or harmful, would
impair in the long run the ability of the state to sustain
the expenditures required to finance the more productive
direct route, especially in an economy with a growing
population. The case for growth to attack poverty cannot therefore be dismissed.

Fallacy 2: *The developmental strategy in India until the
1980s treated growth as a target, as a rival to poverty as a
target, with the latter neglected in consequence.* The anti-
growth sentiment has also followed from elementary
ignorance of the history of developmental planning in
India. Thus, in the 1970s, it became commonplace to
claim that the developmental economists and planners
everywhere had been preoccupied in the 1950s and 1960s
with growth, rather than the alleviation of poverty, as
their objective. This was the central theme of writings on
developmental economics, originating with varying

degrees of explicitness from some academic economists as well as international agencies such as the International Labour Organization.

Let me confess that this contention may be both true and false. I say this, not in the frolic spirit of my good friend, the philosopher Sidney Morgenbesser. On being asked by one of his radical students during the Cultural Revolution whether he thought that Chairman Mao was right in arguing that a proposition could be both true and false, he instantly replied: I do and I don't. Rather, I wish to enter the caveat that developing countries form such a mosaic ranging from city states such as Hong Kong to subcontinents such as China, or from democracies such as India to dictatorships such as yesterday's Chile and Argentina, that one is tempted to agree with Joan Robinson that almost everything is valid somewhere and almost nothing is true everywhere. I must confess that the enormity of this problem was brought home to me when I, coming from India with its population of over 850 million, recently visited Barbados with a population of 250,000. Asked to talk at the Central Bank, I found myself in the Governor's office on the top floor, only to realize that you could practically look out over the whole island. There was evidently no sensible distinction here between partial- and general-equilibrium analysis! So, to shield myself, I reminded my audience of the famous Mao–Nasser story. On a visit to Beijing, Nasser looked unhappy. Concerned, Mao inquired what was wrong. Nasser answered: 'I am having trouble with my neighbours, the Israelis.' 'How many are there?' asked Mao. 'About two million,' Nasser replied. 'Oh!' said Mao, 'which hotel are they staying at?'

I have no doubt that somewhere growth became an objective in itself during the early post-war years. Indeed, it may well have done so in countries where élites identified GNP, and associated size of the national economy, with respectability and strength in the world economy and polity. But, in influential developmental planning circles, GNP was simply regarded as an instrumental variable, which would enable one to impact on the ultimate and central objective of reducing poverty.

In fact, in India the reduction of poverty was explicitly discussed during the late 1950s and early 1960s as the object of our planning efforts.[27] In the Planning Commission, where Pitambar Pant headed the Perspective Planning Division, work was begun at this time on this precise issue. How could we provide 'minimum incomes' for meeting the basic needs of all? The objective being to provide such minimum incomes, or to ameliorate poverty, rapid growth was decided upon as the principal instrument through which this objective could be implemented. Let me explain why we came to focus on growth as the central weapon in our assault on poverty.

I can speak to the issue, as it happens, from the immediacy of personal experience. For I returned to India during 1961, to join the Indian Statistical Institute which had a small think-tank attached to Pant's Division in the Planning Commission. Having been brought in by Pant to work as his main economist, I turned immediately to the question of strategy for minimum incomes. I assembled such income distribution data as were then available for countries around the world, both functional and personal, to see if anything striking could be inferred about the relationship between the economic and political system and policies and the share of the bottom three or

---

[27] Chakravarty, fn. 22, above, ch. 3, documents this and related official analyses of income distribution questions in a thorough fashion. The intellectual antecedents of the widespread focus on poverty alleviation in Indian thinking are discussed with insight by the historian T. Raychaudhuri in his essay, 'Towards a Transformation of Indian Culture: India, 1947–1956' (St Antony's College, Oxford, mimeo, 1991). Also, as T. N. Srinivasan has reminded me, explicit attention to poverty alleviation dates back at least to the National Planning Committee of the Indian National Congress, established in 1938. The 'Bombay Plan', published in 1944 by leading industrialists and businessmen, also had explicit analysis of a 'minimum standard' of living for India's masses and a plan to achieve it. Cf. *A Plan for Economic Development for India*, by P. Thakurdas *et al.* (Harmondsworth: Penguin, 1944).

four deciles. You can imagine the quality of these data then, by looking at their quality now almost a quarter of a century later. Nor did we have then anything systematic on income distribution in the Soviet Union. And admittedly we had nothing on China, which was an exotic reality, about to make its historical rendezvous with the Cultural Revolution, but already suggesting to the careful scholar that its economic claims were not to be taken at face value.

The scanning of, and reflection on, the income distribution data suggested that there was no dramatic alternative for raising the poor to minimum incomes except to increase the overall size of the pie. The inter-country differences in the share of the bottom deciles, where poverty was manifestly rampant, just did not seem substantial enough to suggest any alternative path.[28] The strategy of rapid growth was therefore decided upon, as a consequence of these considerations, as providing the only reliable way of making a sustained, rather than a one-shot, impact on poverty. I must recall a visit to our think-tank by the great Polish economist, Michał Kalecki, whose socialist credentials were impeccable. He told me, while he was working on fiscal policy to raise savings towards accelerated investment: 'Bhagwati, the trouble with India is that there are too many exploited and too few exploiters.'

Growth therefore was indisputably conceived to be an instrumental variable, not as an objective *per se*. It is not surprising therefore that the assertions to the contrary by institutions and intellectuals who belatedly turned to questions of poverty in the 1970s have provoked many of us who were 'present at the creation' to take the

[28] We have learnt since then that income distributions are not so inflexible, of course. For instance, in the United States, the pre-tax and net-of-tax income distribution has been affected significantly during the 1980s, with substantial improvement in the uppermost percentile and deterioration at the bottom. The analysis of the 'structural' reasons why this has happened is currently a major preoccupation of economists.

backward glance and then to turn again to stare coldly and with scorn at these nonsensical claims.

Gilbert Etienne, the well-known sociologist-cum-econ-omist, has exclaimed: 'The claim that development strategies in the 1950s and 1960s overemphasized growth and increases of the GNP at the cost of social progress is a surprising one! . . . Equally peculiar is the so-called discovery of the problem of poverty.'[29] T. N. Srinivasan and B. S. Minhas, both of whom have worked with great distinction on questions of poverty and who fol-lowed me to join Pant's think-tank, have been even more critical. I am afraid that I have also been moved to write in a personal vein: 'on hearing the claim that poverty had only recently been discovered and elevated as a tar-get of development, I fully expected to find that Chapter One of my 1966 volume on *The Economics of Underdeveloped Countries* would be titled Growth; behold my surprise when it turned out to be Poverty and Income Distribution![30]

Fallacy 3: *Growth amounts to a conservative 'trickle-down' strategy*. The most egregious fallacy, however, has been for several economists and ideologues to assume that the growth-oriented indirect route must necessarily be a conservative option. The more liberal and radical among them have therefore tended to rush to their com-puters and their pens each time any evidence suggests that the indirect route may be productive of results, seeking to discount and destroy any such inference.

I have never quite understood this phenomenon. For the growth strategy was conceived by us at the start of our planned assault on poverty as an activist, interven-tionist strategy. The government was to be critically

[29] Cf. G. Etienne, *India's Changing Rural Scene, 1963–1979* (Oxford: Oxford University Press, 1982), 194–5.

[30] Cf. J. Bhagwati, 'Development Economics: What have we Learned?' *Asian Development Review*, 2(1) (1984), repr. in D. Irwin (ed.), *Political Economy and International Trade* (Cambridge, Mass.: MIT Press, 1991), the fifth volume of my collected essays published by MIT Press.

involved in raising internal and external savings, in guiding if not allocating investment, in growing faster so that we could bring gainful employment and increased incomes to more of the poor. Whether the policy framework we worked with in India to use the indirect growth-based approach was an appropriate one, and whether therefore this route was efficiently exploited, is a different but critical issue which I will address in the next chapter.

Since, therefore, the growth strategy was an activist strategy for impacting on poverty, I have always preferred to call it the 'pull-up', rather than the 'trickle-down', strategy. The trickle-down phrase is reminiscent of 'benign neglect' and its use in the first Reagan administration to accompany efforts at dismantling elements of the welfare state has imparted yet other conservative connotations to it. The pull-up phrase, on the other hand, correctly conveys a more radical interventionist image and the intellectual context in which it emerged was defined by the ethically attractive objective of helping the poor.

Thus, growth was seen not as an end in itself, but as arguably the principal (but not the only) means for assaulting India's massive poverty and as indeed offering a radical, interventionist pull-up strategy. To think otherwise is to obfuscate the reality.

I would argue further that the actual experience in India and elsewhere shows that growth can pull people up into gainful work and reduce poverty and, furthermore, that the failure of India's attack on poverty came, not from a mistaken emphasis on growth, but from the inadequacy of growth itself. Poverty persisted because there was little growth, not because growth was the wrong strategic choice.

In the next chapter I shall turn to the analysis of the inefficiencies of India's policy framework that held back India's growth. For the present, I conclude by arguing that, where growth has occurred, it has indeed worked by and large to ameliorate poverty.

International experience

Let me first stress that countries such as South Korea and Taiwan, which have grown much faster than India in the post-war period to date, have had a substantial impact on their living standards. To see the force of the argument, that India's poor growth performance has affected its prospects for raising living standards, it is useful to understand the force of compound interest. 'Had India's GDP grown as rapidly from 1960 to 1980 as South Korea's it would stand at $531 billion today rather than $150 billion—surpassing that of the UK, equal to that of France, and more than twice that of China. India's per capita income would have been $740 instead of $260; even with the benefits of growth inequitably distributed, it is not unreasonable to believe that most of the poor would have been substantially better off.'[31]

Indian experience

Within India too, there is some evidence that growth will reduce poverty.[32] I will cite only a few notable studies from a voluminous literature. In particular, Bagicha Minhas's work in the early 1970s is relevant in having drawn attention to the fact that the incidence of poverty goes down in good harvests and up in years of bad harvests. He has reconfirmed these results in later

---

[31] Cf. M. Weiner, 'The Political Economy of Growth in India', *World Politics*, 38(4) (1986). The contrast becomes even starker if we use the period up to 1990. According to the 1992 *World Development Report* (World Bank, Washington, DC), the average annual growth rate of real GNP per capita during 1965–90 was 1.9% for India and 7.1% for South Korea (p. 218).

[32] I have discussed the evidence at some length in 'Poverty and Public Policy', fn. 26, above. I have drawn on this text of the Vikram Sarabhai Memorial Lecture for some of the arguments above concerning the anti-growth fallacies.

research.[33] Agricultural growth evidently implies less rural poverty.

Then again, Montek Ahluwalia's classic 1978 work on rural poverty and agricultural performance had analysed all-India time-series data to underline this precise link.[34] This work has provoked controversy, with the radical response being provided by Saith, who had drawn the opposite conclusions while working with the same data-set. Analysis of the two papers by Mathur, examining both the econometrics and the economics of the issue, reaches the conclusion, however, that 'aggregate all-India data support Ahluwalia's contention that agricultural growth reduces poverty'.[35]

T. N. Srinivasan, who has raised several objections to the econometric procedures and inferences in Saith's analysis, none the less cautions that Ahluwalia's results, which were further confirmed by him in 1985 by inclusion of additional data which had become available since 1978, should not be treated as an altogether decisive test of the pull-up hypothesis.[36] For the data show that 'there was no upward trend in net domestic product of agriculture per head of rural population—there was very little to trickle-down at the all-India level'. Discussing

[33] Cf. B. S. Minhas, 'Rural Poverty, Land Distribution and Development Strategy', *Indian Economic Review*, 5 NS (1970), 97–126; B. S. Minhas, 'Rural Poverty and Minimal Level of Living: A Reply', *Indian Economic Review*, 6, NS (1971), 69–77; and B. S. Minhas, L. R. Jain, S. M. Kansal, and M. R. Saluja, 'On the Appropriate Choice of Consumer Price Indices and Data Sets for Estimating the Incidence of Poverty in India', *Indian Economic Review*, 1 (1987).

[34] Cf. M. S. Ahluwalia, 'Rural Poverty and Agricultural Performance in India', *Journal of Development Studies*, 14 (1978).

[35] Cf. A. Saith, 'Production, Poverty and Prices in Rural India', *Journal of Development Studies*, 17 (1981), and S. Mathur, 'Rural Poverty and Agricultural Performance in India: A Comment', *Journal of Development Studies*, 23 (1985).

[36] Cf. M. Ahluwalia, 'Rural Poverty, Agricultural Production and Prices: A Re-examination', in J. Mellor and G. Desai (eds.), *Agricultural Change and Rural Poverty: Variations on a Theme by Dharam Narain* (Baltimore, Md: Johns Hopkins University Press, 1985), and T. N. Srinivasan, 'Agricultural Production, Relative Prices, Entitlements and Poverty', in Mellor and Desai, *ibid.*

also the related work by Bardhan, utilizing some state-level data of still less reliability, Srinivasan has concluded that meaningful tests with more and better longitudinal data than have been available are necessary, by regions or areas differentiated by high and low growth rates, before firm conclusions can be drawn on the issue.[37]

The empirical analysis of the link in India between growth and poverty will doubtless continue.[38] But there is little evidence to date establishing for India as a central tendency the worst-case scenarios, possible in theory,[39] where growth bypasses or even harms the poor. I should only add three important propositions to this basic conclusion:

• The growth process can be biased by policy to benefit the poor: e.g. through land reforms, through improvement of access to credit, fertilizers and irrigation, etc. as indeed Indian policy has sought to do from the very beginning of Indian planning.

• Again, as argued in the next chapter, growth may be not merely slow but also distorted, as by an autarkic inward-looking trade policy which favours capital-intensive sectors and discriminates against labour-intensive

---

[37] Cf. Srinivasan, fn. 36, above, and P. Bardhan, 'Poverty and the "trickle-down" in Rural India: A Quantitative Analysis' (mimeo, Berkeley, Calif.: University of California, 1982).

[38] I should draw attention, in particular, to N. Kakwani and K. Subbarao, 'Rural Poverty in India: 1973–87', forthcoming in M. Lipton and J. van der Gaag (eds.), *Including the Poor* (Washington, DC: World Bank, 1993). This study also suggests that 'a positive growth generally tended to reduce the poverty' (p. 52) but also offers nuanced analysis.

[39] The theoretical possibilities of growth that immiserizes people, including paradoxically those who grow, are familiar in the literature on trade theory. Similar paradoxical phenomena resulting from transfers such as foreign aid have also been analysed in the theoretical literature on the transfer problem. For a synthesis and review of the theories of (self-)immiserizing growth and of the related but distinct recipient-immiserizing and donor-enriching transfer paradoxes, see J. Bhagwati, R. Brecher, and T. Hatta, 'The Paradoxes of Immiserizing Growth and Donor-Enriching "Recipient Immiserizing" Transfers: A Tale of Two Literatures', *Weltwirtschaftliches Archiv*, 120(2) (1984), 228–42.

exports, in ways that also affect income distribution and
poverty adversely. Importantly, the nature of growth
matters as much as growth itself.

• Finally, there is likely to be beneficial linkage between
the 'direct' anti-poverty programmes and the 'indirect'
growth strategy. Improved incomes from growth may in
turn improve the ability to obtain access to and exploit
the benefits of the anti-poverty programmes.[40] Growth
should also improve, through the effective 'empower-
ment' provided by economic alternatives, the ability to
get land and other reforms implemented at the ground
level.[41]

But that inadequate growth most be held accountable
as a principal cause of the limited success of India's anti-
poverty efforts, and not simply of her diminished stand-
ing as a role-model for economic policy-making in the
developing world, is an assertion that we can safely
make with about as much plausibility and conviction as
economic analysis can ever generate.

Economists will continue to debate whether resources
should have been shifted at the margin from direct anti-
poverty to indirect (growth-based) anti-poverty programmes. I am myself persuaded that the Indian
planners underestimated the productive role of better
health, nutrition, and education and hence underspent
on them. But it is hard to imagine strong consensus
emerging on this question, since too many imponder-
ables, reflecting unknown relationships among relevant

---

[40] This was suggested by D. T. Lakdawala, 'Planning for minimum needs',
in T. N. Srinivasan and Pranab Bardhan (eds.), *Rural Poverty in South Asia*
(New York: Columbia University Press, 1986), ch. 12.
[41] This has been suggested as a hypothesis by me in *Growth and Poverty*,
Occasional paper No. 5 (Michigan State University Centre for Advanced
Study of International Development, East Lansing, Mich., 1985). The recent
empirical work by K. Subbarao also suggests that 'complementarity' may
indeed obtain between growth and direct anti-poverty programmes in amelio-
rating poverty, whether it is for the Lakdawala argument, see fn. 40, or for
the reason advanced by me.

variables, are involved. But it should be much easier to agree on the different, and far more important question: did we get enough out of whatever we put into each of these two approaches?

In particular, did we get satisfactory growth from our investment?[42] Evidently we did not. So I must now turn to the central question: what went wrong?

---

[42] Doubtless, we must also ask whether we received enough returns from the resources spent on the direct approach and make improvements there continually. There is of course a voluminous and insightful literature on this issue.

2

WHAT WENT WRONG?

The disappointing growth rate over more than a quarter
century, of an annual average of 3.59 per cent in the
1950s, 3.13 per cent in the 1960s, and 3.62 per cent in
the 1970s,[1] must be explained. The Harrod–Domar

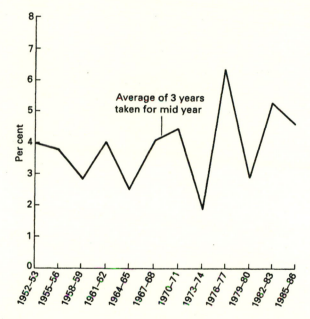

FIG. 2. Growth rates in real GNP in the Indian economy, 1952–86
Source: Government of India.

[1] The moving average of three-year annual growth rates is plotted in Fig. 2,
showing also the fluctuations that reflect, among other things, the agricultural
harvest and its effect on the rest of the economy.

model provides the stylized analytical categories within which this explanation is best provided.

LOW PRODUCTIVITY, NOT INADEQUATE SAVING

In essence, the weak growth performance reflects, not a disappointing savings performance, but rather a disappointing productivity performance. The Indian savings rate more than doubled during this period, from roughly 10 per cent to approximately 22 per cent during 1950–84, supporting a somewhat higher domestic investment rate owing to the (relatively modest) influx of foreign savings, chiefly in the form of assistance rather than foreign investments (Fig. 3). But the growth rates did not step up correspondingly.

There is an interesting parallel with the Soviet Union. The Soviet Union had falling growth rates during the period 1951–80 in the face of high and mildly rising saving rates. The productivity of investments had been abysmal there too, with the effect showing up in falling, not just stagnant growth rates (Fig. 4). On the other hand, in India with rising saving (and investment) rates, the effect of inadequacies in the policy design and framework showed itself in stagnant growth rates.

DISMISSING ALTERNATIVE EXPLANATIONS

But before I consider where exactly the Indian policy framework went wrong, it is necessary to examine more carefully the lack of correspondence between savings and growth rates in India. In particular, there are three possible alternative explanations that must be assessed and dismissed before the inference that I am drawing about the abysmally low productivity of increased savings can be firmly drawn:

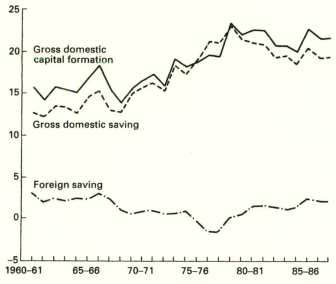

FIG. 3. The financing of gross domestic capital formation by gross domestic saving and foreign saving (as per cent of GDP at market prices)
Note: Negative foreign savings are indicated by a bolder line.
Source: National Accounts Statistics: new series. From V. Joshi and I. M. D. Little, *India: Crisis, Adjustment and Growth*, World Bank mimeo, 1992 (Oxford: Oxford University Press, 1993, forthcoming), ch. 13.

1. Savings may have been overestimated.
2. Income may have been underestimated.
3. The composition of investment may have shifted efficiently towards sectors with greater capital intensity.[2]

There is something to be said for each of these possible explanations, but not much, certainly not enough to make a serious dent on the thesis that low productivity,

---

[2] I deliberately add the proviso 'efficiently' to rule out the possibility that the shift in investment towards more capital-intensive sectors may itself be an inefficiency resulting from faulty policy design. Only those composition shifts which are exogenous to the policy framework must be isolated if they are to be treated as a factor detracting from the thesis of low returns from the increased savings and investment.

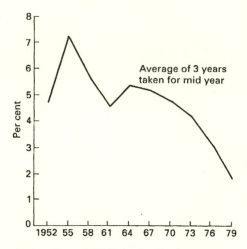

FIG. 4. Growth rates in real GNP in the Soviet economy, 1951–80
Source: P. Desai, *The Soviet Economy: Problems and Prospects*
(Oxford: Basil Blackwell, 1987).

not a failure to raise savings, lies at the core of India's failure. Thus, let me consider each of these three qualifications, in turn.

Overestimated Savings

We know, for instance, that because of shifts in relative prices of capital goods, the real savings and hence investment rates are not as high as a proportion of GNP as the estimated 22–3 per cent estimates at current prices.[3] If this correction is made, as by a Working Group under the Chairmanship of Professor K. N. Raj, the real gross fixed capital formation as a proportion of GDP none the less increased by more than 70 per cent during the

[3] The work of M. K. Rakshit, 'Income, Saving and Capital Formation in India: A Step towards a Solution of the Savings-Investment Puzzle,' *Economic and Political Weekly* 17(14, 15, 16) (April 1982), 561–72, suggests that even the nominal savings may have been overestimated.

period 1950–80, on a very conservative basis (that does not even adjust for quality changes in capital goods over this period, as noted by Mahfooz Ahmed and S. P. Gupta in their dissenting note to the Raj Committee's estimates).[4]

Underestimated Growth

The underestimation of growth is presumably from the growth of the unrecorded, parallel economy. But to turn to this explanation,[5] we would have to assume either that the parallel economy's income is unrecorded more relative to its investment or that, if both are symmetrically unrecorded, the productivity of investment in the parallel economy exceeds that in the recorded, legal economy.

The latter may well be true in so far as the parallel economy escapes the inefficient policy framework. But if this is true, it is an indictment of the policy framework itself and offers no escape from the low-productivity thesis. As for the former argument, that unrecorded investment may be exceeded by unrecorded income, each relative to its corresponding estimate in the legal economy, there is no empirical evidence that I know of. However, recently T. N. Srinivasan and I have considered formally how much such differential undeclared income and investment would have to be to make a significant contribution to explaining the lack of a satisfactory growth rate.[6] Our judgement was that it would have to be a great deal, therefore offering an unlikely escape from the low-productivity thesis.

[4] Cf. Report of the Working Group on Savings, Reserve Bank of India, Bombay, Feb. 1982.
[5] S. Chakravarty, 'Aspects of India's Development Strategy for the 1980's', *Economic and Political Weekly*, 19(26) (1984), 845–52.
[6] Cf. J. Bhagwati and T. N. Srinivasan, 'Indian Development Strategy: Some Comments', *Economic and Politcal Weekly* 19(47) (24 Nov. 1984), 2006–7. This article comments more broadly on Chakravarty, see fn. 5, above.

Compositional Shift

Finally, the compositional shift escape-route also promises little. There are two ways in which this argument has been made:

1. agriculture became more capital-intensive with the Green Revolution;
2. there were shifts within the industrial sector towards capital-using industries.

Sukhamoy Chakravarty has argued that the Green Revolution created demands for capital-intensive production and the use of fertilizers whereas the earlier expansion of agricultural production was based on extensive cultivation of land.[7] However, bringing in more land does not rule out an increase in the capital-output ratio from diminishing returns to investment as less fertile land is brought into cultivation. At the same time, the Green Revolution carried with it a significant increase in overall productivity that could outweigh the simultaneous increase in capital-intensity and reduce the capital-output ratio.[8] Moreover, within industry generally, my former student Isher Ahluwalia has already shown that a disaggregated industry analysis confirms that a falling output-to-capital ratio has afflicted nearly all industry groups, taken individually.[9]

If we further examine technical change, with conventional econometric estimates of overall factor productivity change, T. N. Srinivasan and I had marshalled much evidence that they showed abysmally low technical change through a two-decade period ending in the early

---

[7] Cf. S. Chakravarty, *Development Planning: The Indian Experience*, 1985 Radhakrishnan Lectures (Oxford: Oxford University Press, 1987), 56.

[8] Moreover, the import-substitution policy with respect to fertilizers, and their production in the public sector, avoidably increased the cost of the fertilizers.

[9] Cf. I. J. Ahluwalia, *Industrial Growth in India: Stagnation Since the Mid-Sixties* (New Delhi: Oxford University Press, 1985).

1970s.[10] A thorough analysis by Isher Ahluwalia in 1985 confirmed these findings for the 1970s as well, with some estimates running negative.[11] Her more recent analysis of productivity growth at a detailed level of disaggregation (for sixty-three industries) of the Indian manufacturing sector unambiguously establishes that there was a prolonged and broad-based phase of stagnation in total factor productivity in the manufacturing sector in the 1960s and the 1970s.[12] Industries accounting for almost 60 per cent of the total value added in manufacturing experienced negative 'total factor productivity' growth during this period.

Yet, we still have one last hurdle to cross, at least for the 1970s. Professor K. N. Raj, one of India's most distinguished economists, has argued that the rise in India's capital-output ratio during this period was matched by its rise elsewhere, the common cause being the oil shock of 1973, so that the inference of inefficient resource use resulting from an inappropriate policy framework is not warranted.[13] But I find this argument unconvincing. The macroeconomic consequences of the oil shock led to a serious rise in unemployment and reduced growth in countries so afflicted. But there is little evidence that this happened in Indian industry. Then again, we also know from Bela Balassa's work[14] at the World Bank that economies with a superior policy framework (especially

[10] Cf. J. Bhagwati and T. N. Srinivasan, *India* (New York: Columbia University Press, 1975).

[11] Ahluwalia, fn. 9, above.

[12] Cf. I. J. Ahluwalia, *Productivity and Growth in Indian Manufacturing* (New Delhi: Oxford University Press, 1991). Significantly, the study establishes a turnaround in this respect in the 1980s. Total factor productivity in the manufacturing sector grew at a rate of 3.4% p.a. in the first half of the 1980s compared with no growth in the preceding decade-and-a-half (indeed, a slight decline at the rate of 0.3% p.a.).

[13] Cf. K. N. Raj, 'Some Observations on Economic Growth in India Over the Period 1952/53 to 1982/83', *Economic and Political Weekly*, 19 (13 Oct. 1984).

[14] Cf. Bela Balassa, 'Adjustment to External Shocks in Developing Economies', World Bank Staff Working Paper 472 (Washington, DC: World Bank, 1984).

in regard to outward-orientation in trade), such as South Korea, managed to surmount the adverse effects of the oil shock substantially better than other developing countries, thus showing lower capital-output ratio worsening and returning us therefore to the question of the policy framework after all to explain India's low productivity performance.

WHY LOW PRODUCTIVITY?

Economists typically look for stylized explanations of economic phenomena. Economic theory, which abstracts from detail to concentrate on the essentials, trains us to do so, enabling us to focus on the forest rather than the trees. The philosopher Henri Bergson once remarked that the great advantage of time is that it prevents everything from happening at once. To us economists, the chief virtue of theory, and of associated stylized explanations, is that it enables us to avoid having to consider all explanations, minor and major, at the same time.

The main elements of India's policy framework that stifled efficiency and growth until the 1970s, and somewhat less so during the 1980s as limited reforms began to be attempted, and whose surgical removal is, for the most part, the objective of the substantial reforms begun in mid-1991, are easily defined. I would divide them into three major groups:

1. extensive bureaucratic controls over production, investment, and trade;
2. inward-looking trade and foreign investment policies;
3. a substantial public sector, going well beyond the conventional confines of public utilities and infrastructure.

The former two adversely affected the private sector's efficiency. The last, with the inefficient functioning of public-sector enterprises, additionally impaired the public-sector enterprises' contribution to the economy. Together, the three sets of policy decisions broadly set strict limits to what India could get out of its investment.

While these policies define the major solution to the puzzle of India's disappointing growth, I also would like to draw attention to a phenomenon that has recently been noted and analysed with insight by the political scientist Myron Weiner: namely, India's failure to spread primary education and to raise literacy to anywhere near the levels that many other countries have managed (Fig. 5).[15]

The proximate reason, analysed by Myron Weiner, is that primary education is not compulsory in India, despite widespread belief in India and outside to the contrary. India only has 'enabling' legislation which permits local governments to enforce compulsory primary education; and the legislation has often not been used. Weiner shows persuasively that in other countries that have successfully increased literacy through primary education, the natural desire of parents to use children for work to augment family income has been countervailed in various ways. One, characterizing much of the West, was the shifting attitude to children, a process stretched out over centuries:

As Philippe Aries has documented, childhood was discovered ('invented?') in Europe in the thirteenth century, but it became more significant by the end of the sixteenth and early seventeenth centuries. In the eighteenth century the concept of adolescence, as distinct from that of childhood, emerged. In time, the central concern of the family became its own children. Children became, as Viviana Zelizer has written, 'priceless.' Children were transformed from valuable wage earners to economically useless but emotionally priceless objects. The transformation did not occur without considerable public debate, and while the upper middle classes held this view of their own

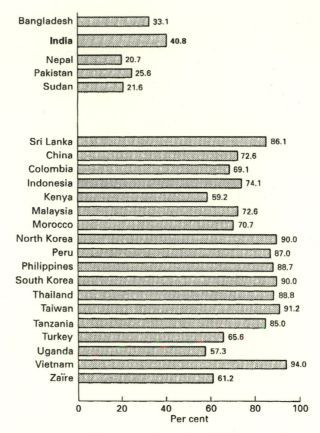

FIG. 5. Rates of literacy of people aged 15 in selected countries in c.1990 (per cent)
Source: M. Weiner, *The Child and the State in India* (Princeton, NJ: Princeton University Press, 1991), Table 7.2.

children they did not readily apply it to the children of the poor.

It was not until the nineteenth century that governments began to regulate the conditions of employment for children and to restrict the ages at which children could work. However, much of the early legislation proved to be ineffective, although the passage of the legislation itself was indicative of changing attitudes toward children and work, and toward the responsibility of the state as protector of children against employers and parents.[16]

Another factor emphasizing the value of basic education, and obtaining in Prussia and Scotland, was the Protestant Reformation. By undercutting the intermediary role of the priesthood between Man and God, it led to the view that everyone should be able to read the Bible, and hence provided the necessary support for primary education by the Church itself.

In India, however, there has been an absence of such countervailing force in favour of primary education. Weiner persuasively documents, from extensive interviews with officials at local levels and in other ways, the pervasiveness of views that reinforce, instead of offsetting, the parental wish to use child labour. These come principally from a caste-defined view of life that undervalues economic and social mobility, and the sense of the futility of educating the children of the poor in an ethos defined additionally by the prevalence of underemployment.

With what we now know about the close relationship between literacy and growth, especially in the context of the Far Eastern economies, though elsewhere too, there seems to me to be little doubt that India's productivity suffered seriously from both the oppressive framework above and the illiteracy below: the pincer movement killing the prospects for efficiency and for growth. I shall concentrate, however, on the framework above, for that defines the agenda for reform that I will address in the final chapter.

The Control of Industry and Trade

Few outside India can appreciate in full measure the extent and nature of India's controls until recently. The Indian planners and bureaucrats sought to regulate both

---

[16] *The Child and the State in India*, 110.

domestic entry and import competition, to eliminate product diversification beyond what was licensed, to penalize unauthorized expansion of capacity, to allocate and prevent the reallocation of imported inputs, and indeed to define and delineate virtually all aspects of investment and production through a maze of Kafkaesque controls. This all-encompassing bureaucratic intrusiveness and omnipotence has no rationale in economic or social logic; it is therefore hard for anyone who is not a victim of it even to begin to understand what it means.

I can illustrate this no better than by recalling the time when I wrote an Op-Ed piece in the *New York Times*, on the occasion of Prime Minister Rajiv Gandhi's first visit to the United States.[17] I was explaining and endorsing the moves towards liberalization of controls, and citing in that context the 'broad-banding' decisions that introduced a limited degree of product diversification. But I had great difficulty getting past an astonished editor, since he simply could not understand what broad-banding meant. When he had finally understood, he asked me whether I could explain why on earth anyone should want to rule out product diversification in the first place.

In essence, the industrial-cum-trade licensing system, whose origin and misguided rationale I shall presently discuss, had degenerated into a series of arbitrary, indeed inherently arbitrary, decisions, where, for instance, one activity would be chosen over another simply because the administering bureaucrats were so empowered, and indeed obligated, to choose. It is tempting to assume 'treason of the clerks', but surely the system was conceived and its rationale initially provided by economists, not by the bureaucrats who by and large were the functionaries entrusted with implementing the system. True,

[17] Cf. J. Bhagwati, 'Is India's Economic Miracle at Hand?', *New York Times*, 9 June 1985.

some of the bureaucrats deluded themselves into believing in the social virtues of a system that gave them these powers and the responsibility to make these arbitrary decisions. Female readers especially will appreciate my recalling a seminar on industrial policy in the Planning Commission in 1967, when I sat next to the economist-bureaucrat in charge of the industrial licensing system. With passion and puritanical zeal, he confronted my criticisms and argued that, without the industrial licensing regime, we would fritter away resources on producing lipstick. As I heard this, I could not help smelling the Brylcream in his hair.

The origins of this bureaucratic nightmare lay, for sure, in the combination of two major factors: first, the inability to trust the market when scarcities are acute and the tasks set are challenging; and second, the failure to understand that markets will generally work better than central planning as a resource-allocational device. The former is a widespread phenomenon, not unique to India. The latter was manifest in the early assertions, from the writings of Barone, Lange, and Lerner, that centralized planning would work better than a decentralized market system because it would calculate prices better. It was left to Hayek to expose the illogicality of this position by arguing that central planners would not be able to secure the information and knowledge that micro-level decision-makers alone would have.[18] Only by ignoring this critical fact, Lange and Lerner were able to prove the proposition that socialism would work better than capitalism, that centralized planning would dominate decentralized markets.

The pernicious role of economic theorizing in other ways, based on what turned out to be wrong premises,

[18] Cf. F. von Hayek, *Knowledge, Education, and Society*, (London: Butler and Tanner, 1983); and his earlier, seminal piece, 'Economics and Knowledge', in his essays, *Individualism and Economic Order* (London: Routledge & Kegan Paul, 1949).

must also be reckoned with if the ideas that led to the comprehensive controls over investment and production are to be accurately assessed. Thus, recall that the Harrod–Domar model was essentially a 'flow' model, ideally assuming a single commodity, and led in practice to policy choices involving both neglect of productivity and attention to savings and hence to fiscal policy and aid policy. The 'structural' models that inherently involved multiple commodities also opened up the question of the ideal allocation of investible resources among alternative uses. There were at least three strands of influential economic argumentation at the time that complemented one another in providing intellectual support for the idea that governmental design and control of investment-allocation decisions was necessary.

Two of them, by Hirschman and by Rosenstein-Rodan, proceeded by formulating the developmental problem as one of creating the inducement to invest but paradoxically wound up by arguing for attending to the composition of investment instead.[19] Hirschman proposed that unbalanced growth characterized the investment process and therefore argued for both the disastrous slash-imports-and-invest policy and the strategy of choosing investments that maximized the inducement to invest by focusing on industries and sectors with maximum forward and backward linkages. By contrast, Rosenstein-Rodan focused on balanced growth in an ingenious argument for co-ordination of decentralized investment decisions, each held up in a Nash equilibrium but made feasible through governmentally-contrived co-operative equilibrium: an idea that has now been elegantly formalized in a

---

[19] Cf. A. Hirschman, *The Strategy of Economic Development* (New Haven, Conn.: Yale University Press, 1958); P. H. Rosenstein-Rodan, 'Problems of the Industrialisation of Eastern and South-Eastern Europe', *Economic Journal* 1943, Vol. 53 and 'Notes on the Theory of the "Big Push" ' (Center for International Studies, Cambridge, Mass.: MIT, 1957), later version in the International Economic Association Conference volume, *Economic Development in Latin America* (London: Macmillan, 1963).

multiple-equilibrium framework by the economists Kevin Murphy, Andre Schleifer, and Robert Vishny.[20] In turn, this implied, in effect, an effort at identifying and guiding the investments to be co-ordinated.

The investment-allocation focus, however, grew more directly out of the subsequent theoretical literature addressed to that problem itself. The combination of the twin assumptions of export pessimism and putty-clay technology implied, in Indian thinking, a shift from the Harrod–Domar to the Feldman–Mahalanobis model where, to match the anticipated shift in future investment, there was need to shift appropriately the investment pattern now. Additional input into this ethos came from the theoretical developments that focused on the heterogeneity of capital goods and the formulation of the optimal trajectory of investments and outputs as in the turnpike theorem. If I may paraphrase Sukhamoy Chakravarty, the logic of investment planning was the order of the day in the high theory of developmental planning.

These ideas thus predisposed the planned effort at development in India, where economists were at the frontier of the developmental thought, towards guidance and control of investments. It was these ideas, bastardized to some extent but not altogether, which led to the institutions (such as the licensing system) which then grew like Frankenstein into the system that I have just described. In turn, these institutions created the interests—the politicians who profit from the corruption, the bureaucrats who enjoy the power, the businesses and the workers who like sheltered markets and squatters' rights—that now pose the threats to change as our ideas themselves have changed and reform is contemplated in light of the new ideas.

The central role of the economists, and their responsi-

[20] Cf. K. M. Murphy, A. Schleifer, and R. Vishny, 'Industrialization and the Big Push', *Journal of Political Economy*, 97 (1989), 1003–26.

bility for India's failings, cannot therefore be lightly dismissed. It is not entirely wrong to agree with the cynical view that India's misfortune was to have brilliant economists: an affliction that the Far Eastern super-performers were spared. There is a related but distinct proposition that India has suffered because her splendid economists were both able and willing to rationalize every one of the outrageous policies that the government was adopting: by ingeniously constructing models designed to yield the desired answers.

The Indian embrace of bureaucratic controls was also encouraged by additional objectives, none of them served well by the control system in practice. One was the prevention of the concentration of economic power, by licensing the creation and expansion of capacity. But, if monopoly power was to be reduced, the virtual elimination of domestic and foreign competition (i.e. the elimination of the 'contestability' of the market) was hardly the way to do it. If the growth of large business houses was to be moderated below what it would otherwise be, that too was not to be: the control system gives better access to the haves than to the have-nots, in practice. But the myth of the efficacy of controls as an anti-monopoly instrument in both these senses remained hard to kill.

Then again, the control system was considered to be necessary to protect the small-scale sector. The large-scale or 'organized' sector, in this view, had to be controlled, its growth restrained by licensing, in order to create space for the small-scale sector. This policy, in fact, made little sense and led to big losses. In an excellent recent analysis, Dipak Mazumdar has shown how this policy handicapped India's successful textile industry.[21] The goal of protecting the hand-looms (household)

---

[21] Cf. D. Mazumdar, 'Import-Substituting Industrialization and Protection of the Small-Scale: The Indian Experience in the Textile Industry', *World Development*, 19(9) (1991), 1197–213. In addition, the official import-licensing

sector created severe problems of competitiveness in international markets for the large-scale sector. The latter was prevented from diversifying into synthetic fibres adequately, for the sake of protecting the small frames producing cotton and the small producers of cotton textiles. Again, expansion into the domestic market was impeded. Mazumdar has correctly observed that:

India has probably been unique in the way it has pursued an import substitution policy of industrialization and also placed severe restrictions on the large-scale industrial sector from expanding in the domestic market for consumer goods. This policy covered a whole range of industries, and the problems discussed in the case of the textile industry have similarly afflicted a number of the others . . . the failure of the large scale industry to exploit the potentially large domestic market—even while its competitiveness in exports was reduced— had a severe dampening effect on economic growth.[22]

But a larger point needs to be made. The attitude that, to protect the small-scale sector, one had to restrain the large-scale sector was symptomatic of a planning approach that presumed that the growth of the large-scale sector would necessarily reduce that of the small-scale sector. This was too mechanistic an approach: quite possibly, the two sectors could have grown together. After all, the soap produced by Lever Brothers is not exactly a substitute for what passes as soap in the small-scale sector. A smarter approach would have been to put in place the machinery to provide assistance to the small-scale sector if its fortunes were indeed affected in reality. In other words, rather than act restrictively on presumed outcomes that no planners could adequately forecast, it would have been sensible to think of an institutional design to cope with adverse consequences were they to materialize.

policy handicapped industry by restricting the importation of superior and more efficient machinery in favour of the domestic equipment manufacturers.

[22] Mazumdar, fn. 21, above, 1211.

Finally, the licensing system was reinforced equally by the fact that regional balance in development was necessary for political, pluralistic, and equity reasons in a multi-state system. But here too the regulatory system of licensed capacity creation, allocating the 'going' capacities 'fairly' among different states at each point of time for each industry, was neither necessary nor desirable. Regional policy can take the form of subsidies, infrastructure, investments, etc. and does not require licensing to redirect investments on a regulated basis. Besides, it was inevitable that the licensing method of allocating investments would degenerate rapidly into politicking by the states to get a share of every bit of licensed capacity. Thus, the small capacities often licensed were split further into yet smaller plants to distribute the largesse over different claimants, accentuating the losses from lack of economic scale. I recall the witty Indian cartoonist R. K. Laxman drawing an irate politician who was complaining that his state had not been allocated a gold mine whereas another had.

If then the comprehensive set of controls over production and investment had many complementary and reinforcing rationales, none of them compelling in their logic and all of them misguided, its costs were certainly considerable. These costs have now been extensively analysed. The stifling of private initiative, the diversion of resources into unproductive rent-seeking activities stimulated by the controls, and costly bottle-necks reflecting artificial rigidities are only illustrative of the unnecessary economic costs imposed by this control-infested system. But the mounting evidence of the system's corrosive influence on the moral ethos and the integrity of political and public life, as corruption was inevitably spawned by politicians and (largely lower-level) bureaucrats tempted to exploit the control system to their advantage, cannot be dismissed from the final accounting of what this regime cost India.

Foreign Trade and Investment

Let me now turn directly to the question of foreign trade and make four observations.

1. Allied to the extensive control framework was India's persistent failure to seize the gains from trade. Indian foreign trade and domestic developmental policies were based on the now outmoded belief in 'export pessimism'. Many countries shared this belief in the 1950s. The great development economists of the time, among them Ragnar Nurkse and Raul Prebisch, accepted this pessimism as well. However, the post-war period showed this pessimism to have been ill-founded.

But while the most successful developing countries adapted their policies in light of the emerging reality of rapidly expanding trade prospects, Indian policies continued to be based on the unrealistic and false premise of export pessimism. The failure to use the exchange rate actively to encourage exports, the inflexibilities introduced by the pervasive controls which must handicap the ability to penetrate competitive foreign markets, the protection and hence attraction of the home market: these policies produced a dismal export performance, while other successful countries expanded their exports rapidly and benefited from greater economic growth. I should perhaps remind you that the architect of India's recent reforms, Dr Manmohan Singh, wrote his D.Phil. thesis at Oxford under Ian Little in 1961, arguing precisely that India's export pessimism was unjustified: but this lesson would be ignored for a long time.[23]

You can gauge the extent to which India failed on the export front by noting that her share in world exports

[23] Cf. M. Singh, *India's Export Trends* (London: Oxford University Press, 1964). This work is the first, systematic analysis of India's export performance (up to 1960, since the thesis was written during 1961) and potential. Since then, there have been other important analyses in the same vein, reinforcing the view that Indian exports could be significantly increased. In particular, see M. Wolf, *India's Exports* (London: Oxford University Press, 1982).

was only 0.41 per cent by 1981, having fallen almost continually since 1948 when it was 2.4 per cent. Fig. 6 shows the dramatic decline that occurred in India's exports relative to both world exports and total developing-country exports. Fig. 7 complements this illustration and underlines further India's dismal export performance by showing an equally dramatic stagnation in her exports–GNP ratio.

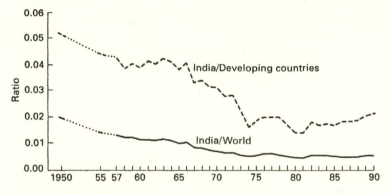

FIG. 6. India's export ratios relative to world exports and developing country exports, 1950–90
Note: Data for 1951–4 and 1956 are missing.
Source: International Financial Statistics, published by IMF.

2. In turn, this surely also reduced India's success with industrialization, not merely with growth. Thus, other countries which began with a much smaller industrial base were not only exporting more manufactures than India but they were also catching up with India in the absolute size of their manufacturing sector. The size of Korea's manufacturing sector, for example, was less than 25 per cent of India's in 1970 (measured at value added). By 1981, it was already up to 60 per cent. Korea's manufactured exports, negligible in 1962, amounted by 1980 to nearly four times those of India. Then again, in 1990 OECD countries imported only $9 billion worth of man-

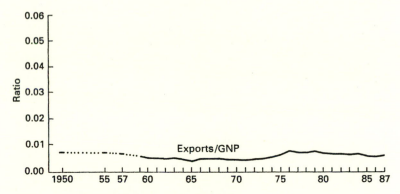

FIG. 7. India's exports/GNP ratio, 1950–87
Note: Data for 1951–4, 1956, and 1958 are missing.
Source: Government of India, New Delhi.

ufactures from India but $41 billion from South
Korea.[24] Simply put, India missed the bus on industrialization during its quarter-century of weak economic performance, (even though, as Fig. A2 in the Statistical
Appendix shows, the share of industry in national
income increased through the four decades since 1950).

In this context, I should perhaps emphasize that rapid
industrialization (based on foreign trade) would also
have facilitated rapid growth by breaking the constraint
that Professors Raj, Chakravarty,[25] and others have continually emphasized as being imposed on the Indian
growth rate by the 'natural' limits on agricultural
growth. These economists have typically argued that
agricultural-growth-based demand constraints operate on
industrial expansion; they also emphasize supply links.
But this argument is only as good as its premise that foreign trade is not available to the economy at the margin.
The premise, however, is unrealistic and must be rejected

[24] Cf. *World Development Report*, 1992 (World Bank, Washington, DC, 1992), 250.
[25] Cf. Chakravarty, fn. 7, above, 60–4.

as one which has done no good to the design of Indian policy.[26]

3. I should also add that the deadly combination of industrial licensing and controls at home with import and exchange controls externally, effectively cut off the rigours of competition from all sources and made the creation of a *rentier*, as against an entrepreneurial, economy more likely. X-inefficiency was certain to follow, with only the exceptional escaping from the consequences of the wrong set of incentives. As Herbert Spencer said eloquently a century ago, 'The ultimate result of shielding men from the effects of folly is to fill the world with fools.'[27]

4. Finally, India's trade and industrial policies handicapped the attack on poverty, not merely by reducing efficiency and growth, but also by distorting its quality. For instance, the capital-intensity of techniques of production in manufacturing was inefficiently increased by the creation of incentives to add to capacity, despite the existence of excess capacity, simply because scarce and profitable imports were allocated to producers pro rata to capacity installed. The exchange control regime also served to eliminate any flexibility in imports of intermediates, parts, etc.: the inability to import these freely increased the incentive to hold inventories, raising both the capital-intensity and lowering the overall efficiency of production.[28] Furthermore, the reliance on capital accumulation as the engine of growth combined with a closed foreign-trade regime implied that India had to

---

[26] A thorough evaluation of the 'demand deficiency' thesis is to be found in T. N. Srinivasan, 'Demand Deficiency and Indian Industrial Development', Yale University (Economics Department), mimeo, forthcoming in a festschrift for K. N. Raj.

[27] H. Spencer, 'State Tamperings with Money and Banks', in *Essays: Scientific, Political, and Speculative*, iii (London: Williams and Norgate, 1891) 354.

[28] These and other inefficiencies were identified and discussed in J. Bhagwati and P. Desai, *India: Planning for Industrialization* (Oxford: Oxford University Press, 1970).

have a relatively larger machinery sector. This added to the capital intensity of her production structure and detracted from the development of labour-intensive manufactures and, ultimately, from a more equitable distribution of income.[29]

Most of all, the inward-orientation of the trade-and-payments regime, in drastically impairing India's export performance, simultaneously prevented the build-up of labour-intensive exports and hence a favourable impact on wages and employment and therefore *ceteris paribus* on poverty as well.[30]

Technology and Direct Foreign Investment

India cannot be faulted much on her technological and scientific achievements. She has to her credit remarkable triumphs shared only with a few, often only advanced nations. She has picked up nodules from the depths of the oceans, put men in Antarctica, fired intermediate missile rockets, won Nobel Prizes in the sciences, and has perhaps the highest number of scientific and skilled people in the developing world.

Yet, as in the Soviet Union, the state of her average technology in the communications and industrial sectors has fallen seriously behind that of the superior performers. While this remains a grey area within Economics, it would be astonishing if, again as in the Soviet Union, excessive controls hindering the freedom to produce or invest, and hence to profit from innovation, have not

---

[29] Cf. A. Panagariya, 'Indicative Planning in India: Discussion', *Journal of Comparative Economics*, 14 (1990), 736–42.

[30] It is ironic that experience has not been kind to the branch of developmental thinking, fashionable in Indian academic circles in the 1950s and 1960s, which favoured the choice of capital-intensive processes and industries on the ground that they would lead to more savings, greater growth, and higher employment later despite lower employment now. For important cross-country evidence on the role of trade and industrial policies on employment and income distribution, see the synthesis volume by A. Krueger, *Trade and Employment in Developing Countries: Synthesis and Conclusions*, NBER (National Bureau of Economic Research) (Chicago: Chicago University Press, 1982), based on several in-depth country studies.

impeded technological innovation.[31] At the same time, the controls on trade have evidently reduced the ability to invest in newer-vintage capital goods embodying technical change.

The restrictions on incoming direct foreign investment have also reduced the absorption of new technology from this source. While the Korean and the Japanese growth of domestic technological capabilities was not based on direct foreign investment, these nations did not have the baggage of India's regime of 'don'ts' that also reduced other forms of technical absorption and innovation. India therefore lost on all counts when it should have, with better policies, gained on them all.

The Public Sector

What I have said so far pertains mostly to the productivity of the private sector. The framework I described, and the consequences I have detailed, were applicable mainly to the private sector, though not entirely since the public sector could not be shielded from most of their problems despite efforts in that direction. But the story in India would not be complete if the public sector, with its special (though perhaps universal) problems, were excluded from scrutiny.

In India, the public sector is truly substantial. From the beginning, no doubt as a consequence of the influence of socialist doctrines on Prime Minister Jawaharlal Nehru and indeed on many of us who studied Economics at Cambridge and Politics at the London School of Economics, the public sector was considered to be an important sector to cultivate and enlarge. Fabianism, with its anti-revolutionary thrust, probably helped define a policy of gradualism: nationalizations were not contemplated but it was expected instead that

[31] Cf. J. Berliner, *The Innovation Decision in Soviet Industry* (Cambridge, Mass.: MIT Press, 1976).

increasing shares of investment in the public sector over successive Five-Year Plans would steadily increase the average size of the public sector to a decisive share in the nation's capital stock. A measured and slow-paced ascent up the Marxist mountain was therefore part of the ideological agenda.

In turn, the two Industrial Policy Resolutions of 1948 and 1956 shifted a number of industries to the exclusive domain of the public sector. Thus the 1956 Resolution stated:

In the first category there will be industries the future development of which will be the exclusive responsibility of the state. The second category will consist of industries, which will be progressively state-owned and in which the state will therefore generally take the initiative in establishing new undertakings, but in which private enterprise will also be expected to supplement the effort of the state. The third category will include all the remaining industries, and their future development will, in general, be left to the initiative and enterprise of the private sector.[32]

The first category turned out to be an enormous one, embracing not merely defence-related industries but also atomic energy, iron and steel, heavy machinery, coal, railways and airlines, telecommunications, and the generation and distribution of electricity. These industries provide the bulk of the infrastructure of the country; their inefficiency could thus, in turn, create inefficiencies in the user-industries in the private sector. It did, as I argue presently.

In fact, the overwhelming presence of the public sector in India must be spelled out to see why the matter of its functioning is of great importance to Indian productivity and economic performance. Thus, the 244 economic enterprises of the central government alone, excluding the

---

[32] Quoted in T. N. Srinivasan, 'Reform of Industrial and Trade Policies', *Economic and Political Weekly* (14 Sept. 1991), 2143–5. For greater detail, see Bhagwati and Desai, fn. 28, above.

What Went Wrong?

railways and the utilities, employed as many as 2.3 million workers in 1990. In manufacturing, if the small 'unorganized' sector is excluded, their employment was over 40 per cent of that provided by the private-sector firms. In fact, the public-sector enterprises in manufacturing, mining, construction, transport and communications, banking and insurance (both now nationalized, partly and wholly respectively), when state-level enterprises are counted in, provided nearly 70 per cent of the 26 million jobs in the large-scale 'organized' sector in 1989.[33]

Not merely because of its size, but also, as I have just noted, because of its composition, which is such that it can affect the supply of important productive inputs such as electricity, transportation, finance, insurance, and steel, and hence influence the efficiency of the private sector, the public sector must be efficient. But, as virtually everywhere to some degree or the other, this has not been the case in India either.[34]

Overstaffing due to politics,[35] the 'goofing-off' effect of soft budget constraints, etc. have been amply documented by a series of investigations. I must confess that I was among the many who thought in the 1950s and 1960s that the public-sector enterprises could be operated better. Recall that this was also the assumption

---

[33] Cf. the excellent account in B. R. Nayyar, 'The Public Sector in India: The Dialectics of Legitimation and Rent Seeking', in L. Gordon and P. Oldenberg (eds.), *India Briefing 1992*, The Asia Society (Boulder, Colo.: Westview Press, 1992). Also note that the share of public-sector to private-sector employment in the 'organized' sector has increased steadily since 1960–1 and sharply in the 1980s, as shown in Fig. A3 in the Statistical Appendix.

[34] Below, I detail some of the reasons for public-sector inefficiency. This is, of course, compatible with the existence of some remarkably successful public-sector enterprises.

[35] There was not merely overstaffing; workers earned wages for overtime too. Indeed, many workers came to believe that their salaries were rewards simply for being employed while, for the work they did, they had to be paid an overtime. This idea was pushed to its limits when even workers of a 'sick unit', no longer in operation, began to ask for a 'notional' overtime. If the unit had been functioning, they reasoned, they would have been receiving an overtime. The same should be paid in addition to the salaries because it was not their fault that the unit had been closed.

underlying the Lange–Lerner argument, now seen to be a consequence of unrealistic premises, that centralized planning would function better than the decentralized market system as an allocative device. In reality, the conditions that would make the public sector productive and efficient seem beyond reach, at least in India.

This inefficiency, directly observed and documented, is not the only cause of public-sector losses, and some of the losses are attributable also to a governmental policy of taking over so-called 'sick units' (i.e. private firms making losses) to respond to political demands for the avoidance of bankruptcy. It is noteworthy, however, that the public-sector enterprises have as a rule produced abysmally low returns on the enormous amounts of employed capital. Thus, even during the decade of the 1980s, when the awareness of the issue was keen, the (simple) average rate of financial return on employed capital was 2.5 per cent! And that too was heavily weighted by the profits of 14 petroleum enterprises which produced as much as 77 per cent of the 1989–90 profits. Besides, even this meagre profitability was ephemeral, based on historical-cost depreciation: corrected for replacement cost, the profits in public-sector enterprises in coal, steel, fertilizer, power, and transport were even estimated to be negative.[36]

But the public sector's economic inefficiency represents only the microeconomic aspect of its failure. The low profitability also amounted to a macroeconomic failure. And this would contribute to the fiscal and foreign exchange crisis that developed in the 1980s, gathering storm at the end of the decade, forcing India into near-bankruptcy and therewith into IMF loan support and the drastic macroeconomic and microeconomic reforms that the present government has firmly embarked upon.

The failure of the public-sector enterprises to generate

[36] Cited in Nayyar, fn. 33, above; see esp. Table 4.

What Went Wrong?

profits and hence contribute to governmental saving coincided with an unprecedented increase in the 1980s of budgetary expenditure on defence, governmental wages and salaries, and subsidies. As a result, the government's contribution to total savings fell dramatically through the 1980s (see Fig. 8). The government had to resort to a mix of increased domestic and foreign borrowing and to reduce simultaneously the growth of capital expenditure which, in fact, declined a little during the 1980s as a proportion of GDP.

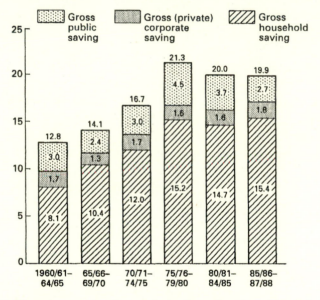

Fig. 8. The components of gross domestic savings in India: period averages (per cent of GDP at market prices)
Source: Same as for Fig. 3.

The relative decline in capital expenditure meant of course that there was a slowdown in the investment in infrastructure. Coming on top of the inefficient use of this investment, this slowdown contributed to the infrastructural bottlenecks that in turn contributed to the low productivity of investment in many user-industries that I noted earlier.

The Crisis

The state of Indian public finances reached crisis proportions by the end of the 1980s. The public debt-to-GNP ratio increased through the 1980s, jumping drastically towards the end of the decade to nearly 60 per cent, a near doubling of the ratio in 1980 (Fig. 9). As I argued above, this had to do with the failure of the public sector to generate investible resources and the explosive growth of governmental current spending that saw the budget deficit as a proportion of GDP rise from 6.4 to 9 per cent during the 1980s.

The two OPEC shocks of 1973 and 1979 had little role to play in this drama. The external shock administered

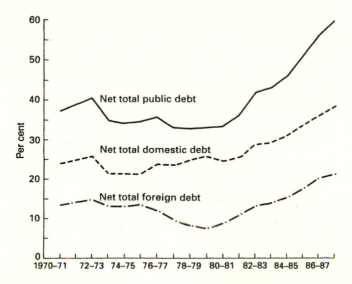

FIG. 9. India's net public debt to GNP ratios, 1970–87
Source: W. Buiter and U. Patel, 'Debt, Deficits, and Inflation: An Application to the Public Finances of India', *Journal of Public Economics*, 47 (1992), 171–205.

by the loss of remittances and the expenditures incurred to rescue workers in the aftermath of the invasion of Kuwait in August 1990 certainly accentuated the fiscal crisis at the end. But the crisis was almost entirely 'home-made'.[37]

The rise in foreign borrowing was a major component of the fiscal crisis. The external public-sector debt as a proportion of GNP doubled during the 1980s to 21 per cent by 1987/8. In consequence, debt service as a proportion of exports increased more than threefold to 32 per cent in 1986-7 from only seven years earlier. The foreign exchange reserves fell through the last three years of the decade. The result was an unprecedented downgrading of India's credit rating in the international capital market.

By 1990 there was palpable fear of default. In January 1991 the government was forced to take IMF loans worth $1.8 billion by drawing from the Compensatory and Contingency Financing Facility and the first tranche of the standby facility. By October 1991 the borrowing was increased under instruments that entailed commitments and firm action both to control and reduce the budget deficit and to undertake structural reforms.

The content of the structural-reform conditionality was no more than what many in India had long seen to be necessary. The reaction of some that these were alien ideas being imposed by the World Bank and the IMF on India was ludicrous. These ideas had been evolved by some of us (and by some foreign economists as well) in the 1960s[38] and had in fact made their way into these

---

[37] This is the adjective used by W. Buiter and U. Patel, 'Debt, Deficits and Inflation: An Application to the Public Finances of India', *Journal of Public Economics* 47 (1992), 171–205. I draw here on their excellent analysis of what went wrong with India's public finances. There is also a splendid treatment of the subject in V. Joshi and I. M. D. Little, *India: Crisis, Adjustment and Growth*, World Bank mimeo, 1992 (Oxford: Oxford University Press, 1993, forthcoming).

[38] The earliest Indian economists include T. N. Srinivasan, V. K. Ramaswami, and Padma Desai. The foreign economists include, among others, Bela Balassa, Arnold Harberger, Anne Krueger, and Ian Little.

institutions which are distinguished for the absorption and diffusion of new and important ideas rather than for their creation.[39] Those denouncing alien intrusion were in fact denying the credit to their own nationals who had contributed to the evolution of the ideas whose serious implementation was now to be India's principal challenge. Also, the structural reform agenda endorsed by the IMF and the World Bank was little different from what the new government of Prime Minister Narasimha Rao had already announced by way of reforms in July 1991, albeit with the foreknowledge and complicity of these multilateral institutions whose lending was imminent.

India was finally at a critical turning-point. The question was no longer: whether reforms? Rather the questions now were: in what sequence, with what speed, with what chance of success? These are issues that lend themselves more to speculation than to serious scholarship. And yet one can use scholarship to gain insights that make the speculation nuanced and informed, as I shall now attempt to do.

[39] This is, of course, as it should be. The universities are naturally the major source of innovation in economics. The evolution of the monetarist approach to the balance of payments by Jacques Polak, and the influential theoretical work of Marcus Fleming and Robert Mundell, at the IMF nearly a quarter-century ago, are among the exceptions that underline this rule.

3

WHAT IS TO BE DONE?

The cure is defined by the diagnosis. The reforms that
needed to be undertaken in the Indian economy were
mainly in her microeconomic framework, requiring the
'structural' reforms that would free the economy and
improve its functioning in ways that are manifest from
the analysis I offered in Chapter 2. But the reforms were
precipitated by the macroeconomic crisis whose origins
and dimension I also sketched.

The macroeconomic crisis, of course, cannot be totally
separated from the microeconomic failings. The failure
to produce adequate returns from public enterprises both
contributed to low income and growth and helped to
create the fiscal crisis by undermining public savings.
The low growth, again, handicapped a more rapid and
effective execution of the pull-up strategy, prompting
possibly the expansion of public-sector and governmental employment and therewith the explosion of the wages
component of the fiscal budget and the deficit. Indeed,
the interconnectedness of the old microeconomic inefficiencies and the new macroeconomic problems has yet
other dimensions, which the Oxford economists Vijay
Joshi and Ian Little have explored ingeniously in their
important recent volume on India's macroeconomic history.[1]

[1] Cf. V. Joshi and I. M. D. Little, *India: Crisis, Adjustment and Growth*
(World Bank, mimeo, 1992; Oxford: Oxford University Press, 1993, forthcom-
ing). See also D. Khatkhate, 'National Economic Policies in India', in
D. Salvatore (ed.), *National Economic Policies* (*Handbook of Comparative
Policies*, i; New York: Greenwood Press, 1991).

Yet, one must recognize that the macroeconomic crisis of the 1980s had its principal origins in forces whose connection to the microeconomic framework is negligible. The weakening of the hold of the Congress Party and the entry of successive and short-lived coalition governments on the political scene must surely account for the corresponding weakening of the state and its fiscal discipline: greater political turnover must surely have prompted expedient spending on a larger scale and with greater frequency. It may be that the Congress Party would not have weakened if India had prospered through better microeconomic policies; but it is foolhardy to assume a necessarily benign relationship between good economic outcomes and the political fortunes of those who produce them.

In any event, it seems eminently plausible that the 'soft state' that Gunnar Myrdal feared may have arrived in the 1980s, precipitating the elimination of the celebrated macroeconomic discipline for which India had earlier been known (as evidenced by the remarkably low rate of inflation up to the 1980s, as seen from Fig. 10).[2] Equally, the civil service appears uncharacteristically to have failed to sound the alarm on the growing fiscal crisis. Did it fall asleep on the watch or did it not act out of growing impotence and prudence in an atmosphere of greater political turnover and hence ambiguities of the proper civil-service role (the two rival models consisting in professing 'commitment' and 'loyalty' to the Minister bent on expedient expenditure or acting as the custodian of the common good)? These considerations will have to be assessed in speculating on the likely success of the reforms that must be undertaken to return India to her conventional, conservative, and sound macroeconomic management of the economy.

Then again, the fact that the microeconomic reforms

---

[2] Fig. 10 shows both the low rate of inflation in India and also the higher rates of inflation in the developing countries altogether.

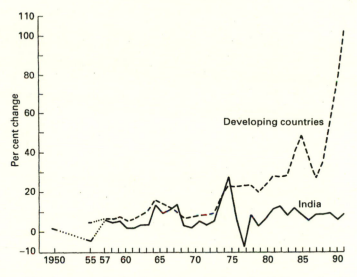

Fig. 10. A comparison of consumer prices in India and other developing countries, 1950–90 (per cent change over previous year) *Source*: International Financial Statistics, published by IMF.

must be undertaken simultaneously now with the macroeconomic stabilization complicates the task of microeconomic reform. The difficulties that would attend microeconomic reform, as competition is introduced and inevitably some must lose as others gain, are greatly compounded by the additional adjustment problems that are entailed by the slamming on of monetary and fiscal brakes to restore macroeconomic stability. And yet, it is hard to imagine that the microeconomic reforms now being undertaken would have been attempted with serious resolve unless there had been a compelling crisis, such as the macroeconomic crisis at the end of the 1980s, that would clear the economic and political fog and permit a clear view of the inefficiencies of India's microeconomic policies. The liberalizing reforms tentatively begun at the end of Mrs Gandhi's life, and pursued somewhat more energetically by Rajiv Gandhi but coming to naught within a year, were both undertaken for reasons other than because these Prime Ministers were looking down the barrel of a gun. For that very reason, among others I shall presently discuss, they were partial and halting, unlike the ones we currently see. And indeed, for that reason, the new reforms are likely to endure even though the solution to the macroeconomic crisis greatly increases the difficulty of successful reform.

MORE ON THE CRISIS

India's economic crisis in the late 1980s was so compelling that a little more needs to be said to underline how its relentless build-up had led to frenetic attempts by successive governments to cope with it, even prior to the current reforms.

Thus in October 1990, the National Front government had imposed a 25 per cent surcharge on petroleum products to reduce the fiscal deficit and also to curb import demand. A new 7 per cent surcharge was also imposed on the corporate tax, doubling it to 15 per cent. In December 1990 the successor Janata Dal government had introduced several additional fiscal measures in a further move to cut the deficit. Both these sets of fiscal measures, it should be stressed, were outside the conventional pattern of annual budgets and, together, they amounted to an emergency programme to reduce the budget deficit directly by 1.5 per cent of GNP.

Simultaneously, there were direct attempts at cutting the payments deficit through the conventional techniques of making imports more expensive through depreciation of the dirty-floating Rupee and the use of cash-margin requirements and restraints on commercial credits for imports.

By the time that the government of Prime Minister Rao took power in June 1991, after the resignation of the Janata Dal government in March had precipitated the elections, these emergency measures had yielded little in the way of concrete results. In fact, any attempt to build on the fiscal and foreign exchange measures of October and December 1990 had been aborted by the policy paralysis as the country was plunged into the politics of elections (and the further unpredictability and fear of instability introduced by the assassination of Rajiv Gandhi in May).

The Compulsions of the Crisis

In an altogether unprecedented fashion, therefore, the new minority government confronted a major decision. Without recourse to further foreign funds to moderate the costs of adjusting out of the serious macroeconomic crisis, the political costs of recovering stability were simply too high. But then these funds could not be procured without finally undertaking the reforms that had proven elusive so far. This situation resulted from a number of factors:

• India's credit rating had collapsed and could not be revived without the reforms. Thus private borrowing was not a realistic alternative in the absence of the reforms.

• The inflows of funds from workers' remittances from the Middle East had also dried up after the Kuwait crisis.

• The reliance on inflows *via* deposits made by non-resident Indians had also shown sensitivity to the possible consequences of India's inability to cope with the crisis: these NRI deposits had started to be withdrawn in the first half of 1991.

• There could again be no relief from the influx of equity funds under direct foreign investment (DFI): the lack of inducement for DFI was part of the inefficient framework requiring reform. In fact, the inflow of DFI had sunk to negligible levels in the years immediately preceding the crisis: in 1988–9 it was an astonishingly low Rs. 183 million; in 1989–90 it was Rs. 210 million; and in 1990–1 it would again be only Rs. 245 million: sums that would barely finance more than a dozen small- to medium-scale projects annually in modern industry!

In addition to these factors specific to India, several major international developments contributed to the situation where it was virtually impossible to win aid without reform.

1. The former Soviet Union turned from a superpower into a superbeggar. This and the associated mushrooming of aid demands for the Soviet Union represent an enormous potential diversion of aid funds from the poor countries at a time of growing world shortage of capital. This diversion of funds from the poor countries of Africa and Asia, with much poverty and great need, to the peoples of the Commonwealth of Independent States is motivated principally by two factors. The first is the fear of relapse into Communism without the aid. Ironically, the last country successfully to get aid by using the argument that it would otherwise go communist has turned out to be the country that first went communist. Equally, there is a fear of anarchy, prompting nuclear fall-out and refugee outflows.

These are powerful reasons driving the regrettable diversion of massive funds away from the poor countries. To Mr Nixon's accusatory and galvanizing cry of 'who [will have] lost Russia?', there is no effective response by anyone arguing 'who will have found India?' The principle of enlightened self-interest, which always works more effectively than altruism, favours the diversion of funds to the former Soviet Union, making the work of getting aid for India's needs ever more difficult. Lest you doubt the power of enlightened self-interest, let me tell you the story of the rich man and the poor man who were praying in church. The rich man said: 'Dear God, I need a million dollars to help me with my leveraged buyout.' Next the poor man said: 'Oh God, please grant me a loaf of bread or I will die of starvation today.' At which point, the rich man opened his wallet, took out a hundred dollars and thrust them into the pauper's hands, saying: 'Take that money and buy yourself all the bread you can eat; but for Christ's sake shut up, for I need the Lord's undivided attention.'

2. But if aid funds for the poor countries were getting scarce, owing to these new and big claims on them, they were under pressure also because of increased demands in the United States for domestic spending on education, on the inner cities, etc. and for reduction in the budget deficit without increased taxation.

3. The shrinking funds were therefore increasingly geared, both bilaterally and (because of weighed voting) multilaterally, to a demonstration of willingness to use them to advantage. A shrinking budget led to greater attention to efficiency of use.

4. In turn, this dovetailed into the worldwide collapse of older attitudes and policies broadly supportive of the anti-DFI, inward-looking, inappropriately regulatory and pro-public-sector policies of the kind that India had embraced to an extreme degree. Not merely had the former communist regimes and former communists such as Mikhail Gorbachev and Boris Yeltsin abandoned these policies and the attendant ideology and rhetoric. So had nearly all of South America, equally under a macroeconomic crisis (induced by the excessive borrowings of the 1970s).

India thus faced a changed world, where many claimants were in line for scarcer aid funds, ahead of India with the kinds of reforms that had now become synonymous with efficiency of use and hence with aid-worthiness. If she wished to tap the traditional bilateral and also multilateral sources of external aid funds, she really had little alternative to embracing the long-delayed reforms.

But the reforms cannot wholly be put down to this set of crisis-induced compulsions. The necessity for the microeconomic reforms had been steadily, if ever so slowly, understood more widely through the 1980s. Tentative moves towards delicensing had been planned as early as towards the end of Mrs Gandhi's term before her assassination, in the wake of a series of official examinations of the licensing and tax regimes. But, with her formative years spent in an intellectual atmosphere permeated with the Fabian thinking that characterized her father's world-view, I suspect that Mrs Gandhi would have been a reluctant reformer, at best. It is in fact hard to imagine that she would have proceeded steadily further down the road to liberalization if she had not been assassinated: somehow this scenario seems wholly out of character with her past thought processes, her acute experience of political difficulties following upon the June 1966 devaluation and liberalization over which she presided soon after her first becoming Prime Minister, and her occasional political successes following upon socialist (not liberalizing) policies such as bank nationalization. We will never know; but any speculation suggesting continued reforms by her cannot really be supported by cogent arguments.

Instead, Rajiv Gandhi was manifestly for the reforms when he took office in the aftermath of Mrs Gandhi's assassination and proceeded to return to office with the greatest majority obtained by any Prime Minister in an Indian election. His reforms were less cautious, more explicit, and sprang from a distinct sense of their utility and necessity. The reason was not just the absence of the socialist baggage: cynics suggested that his lack of cerebral interests precluded, in any event, the possibility of an intellectual vision, even if flawed. There was, in my judgement, an intuitive grasp of the costs that the vast control apparatus, in particular, was imposing on the country.

When I saw him soon after he assumed elective office, he told me animatedly how he planned to remove the heavy hand of bureaucracy that lay over all activities. Not merely would licences go but also 'Vice-Chancellors will no longer have to wait for days in the corridors of the Education Ministry, trying to see a joint secretary.' Some have put this infusion of pragmatism down to genes on his father's side: Parsis have the double advantage of humour and common sense. But I believe it really had to do with the fact that Rajiv Gandhi, a former pilot with the Indian Airlines, was the first Prime Minister to have done honest work outside politics. He thus had seen for himself, and through his friends, the system that he sensibly deplored and would seek to change. It really makes all the difference how you see the control system, whether from the lens of the one who runs it or of the one whom it runs over. The wise Nobel-laureate economist Arthur Lewis, adviser to Hugh Gaitskell, is supposed to have gone up to Thomas Balogh, later adviser to Prime Minister Harold Wilson, and said: 'Tommy, the difference between your socialism and mine is that when you think of socialism you think of yourself as behind the counter whereas when I think of socialism I think of myself as being in front of it.'

Rajiv Gandhi's intuitive support for reforms was matched by his Finance Minister V. P. Singh's grasp at the time of their importance. The effectiveness of this team was reflected in the shrewd pursuit of tax reforms which, in increasing yields when income tax rates were reduced, demonstrated quickly that pragmatic moves towards reform were sensible. This early and visible success, unimportant objectively in a country where income tax is paid only by a minuscule fraction of the economically active population, was subjectively of great significance. For, in creating visible success, it earned credibility for the reform effort and hence bought the time necessary to implement the more difficult reforms in the far more pervasive and persistent control framework.

Rajiv Gandhi's reforms were hardly revolutionary in conception or in execution. In retrospect, they amounted to an acquiescence in the regime but a mild attempt at moderating its worst excesses. They were a small step in the right direction; they generated enthusiasm simply because India seemed finally to be going down the right road.

It has become customary to signal the changes at the Budget sessions of the Parliament. Rajiv Gandhi's main reforms were also announced at the annual 1985 Budget session. The main reforms were in industrial licensing and regulatory policies.

Twenty-five industries were delicensed. However, traditional problems still continued for them with regard to licensed imports of equipment, clearance from the Monopolies and Restrictive Trade Practices (MRTP) Commission, inability to function if the small-scale sector reservation policy applied, and similar restrictions that had grown up around the Indian industrial regime. Besides, most of the industrial sector did not benefit from even this restricted version of delicensing.

The restrictions on product diversification were relaxed through 'broad-banding' products among which the licensed producer of any one of the banded products could switch production. But again, the relaxation was confined to cars, machine-tools, paper, and parts of electrical machinery: the broad-banding applying to specified products within each industry rather than freely across these industries. This helped but surely left most of the problem untouched, the scope of the action being minuscule in itself.

There were minor relaxations in regard to MRTP's scope as well. The exemption limit for asset size qualifying for MRTP scrutiny was raised fivefold, restoring it to what it had been in 1969 (when the Commission was established) in real terms. The result was almost to halve the number of industrial 'houses' that would qualify for MRTP approval for capacity-expanding investments.[3]

Alongside these improvements, there were minor improvements in tax policy, in small-scale-sector reservation policy, in industrial policy to allow the private sector to enter into telecommunications equipment manufacturing, and in other ways.

The improvements continued through the year and were followed by more policy changes in the March 1985 Budget session, chiefly in the shape of further exemptions from MRTP approval reducing the afflicted companies to nearly 15 per cent of the earlier total, and an expansion of the broad-banding privileges to a few other industries.

Admittedly, from the perspective of the ardent reformers, all this activity did not amount to a hill of beans. But it would be wrong to infer that the reforms had not generated an air of expectancy, a hope of more to come of a change that would take root and grow stronger. The team of Prime Minister Gandhi and his Finance Minister V. P. Singh seemed politically in charge, united in purpose, and dedicated to the reform of India's economy.

In the end, however, the team broke up over the Bofors scandal and the Watergate mentality that overcame the beleaguered Prime Minister.[4] The scandal itself was undoubtedly a (possibly inevitable) consequence of the corruption, or of the pervasive sense of corruption, that the control system had created. In leading the Prime Minister, under the advice of his palace guard, to expel

---

[3] Even here, however, the changes do not appear to have been uniformly liberalizing: the 1984 legislative changes in MRTP operation appear to have had some deliberalizing effects as well.

[4] The scandal concerned the allegation that there had been pay-offs in the purchase of Bofors guns from Sweden, with allegations that the beneficiaries included the top leadership of the government and the Congress Party.

spawned the political schisms that led to the political instability that quickly put the reforms on hold. Astonishingly, the Prime Minister's entourage were even foolish enough to attack V. P. Singh as the architect of 'reactionary' economic policies, thus seeking to distance Rajiv Gandhi from the reforms and consequently throwing the baby out with the bath water.[5]

The reforms had thus come to naught. They would not now be attempted vigourously until the election of the Rao government several years later. But, as the late 1980s unfolded, the sentiment among intellectuals and economists moved steadily in the direction of reform. While a few of us had been arguing for the reforms since the mid-1960s, we were then in virtual isolation. By the mid-1980s, especially after Rajiv Gandhi's early reforms had broken the ice, many were coming into our corner. Thus, the distinguished policy-maker I. G. Patel, who had by then become the Director of the London School of Economics, ironically used the occasion of a lecture in memory of the great Fabian Kingsley Martin to urge that a bonfire of industrial licenses was in order.[6]

In fact, the sentiment for reforms had spread increasingly among the general population. The control system, known popularly as the unpopular 'permit raj', touched many at a multitude of points. Admittedly, many learnt to bribe, evade, avoid, and generally live with the system. But it remained a thorn in one's side, a continuing reminder of an economic system out of control and a political system out of bounds. The time was ripening when an assault on the system would be greeted with a sense of relief.

This change of mood could also be read in the plat-

---

[5] Statements to this effect were attributed in the press at the time to trusted lieutenants in the cabinet.

[6] Cf. I. G. Patel, 'On Taking India into the Twenty-First Century (New Economic Policy in India)', 15th Kingsley Martin Memorial Lecture, *Modern Asian Studies*, 21(2), 1987.

This change of mood could also be read in the platforms of the political parties, other than the communists, during the elections that returned Prime Minister Rao to power and government. While there were many ambiguities and differences, there was little support in the platforms against economic reforms. The status quo was simply not on anyone's agenda.

But, most of all, the psychology of the leadership that took power in June 1991 must provide the ultimate compulsion for the reforms unleashed by it. The internationally informed Indian élite had surely come to appreciate the extent to which India's voice had been marginalized in world economic affairs as her economy and her policies became increasingly matters of indifference to others. The worst psychological state to be in is to have a superiority complex and an inferior status. This incongruity cried out to be fixed: reforms were increasingly seen to be the only answer.

Then again, for both the Prime Minister and the Finance Minister, who masterminded the reforms, the reward of successful reform may be a place in history. The reward of returning to business as usual, once the macroeconomic crisis is tackled, is just a footnote in the history textbook. The two are making waves; they can ride them into glory and gratitude from their compatriots. As Mikhail Gorbachev once remarked, he could have continued like Brezhnev and led a quiet life; but he chose the difficult path. And he made history. Prime Minister Rao and Finance Minister Mammohan Singh expect no less, though I suspect they hope for less turbulence than Gorbachev and his Soviet Union ran into.

All of these factors provide the countervailing force to contain the opposition that threatened interests will inevitably provide in the political arena. To understand these interests and their strength, however, it is necessary to see what the reforms to date have been and where they are headed.

THE REFORMS

There are two main features of the reforms that are dramatically different from the efforts in earlier episodes (under Mrs Gandhi and Rajiv Gandhi);[7] and both strengthen the chance of success. First, the reforms are forceful and explicit. The direction is clearly set, and there is no ambiguity of intention. This was not true to the same degree even in Rajiv Gandhi's abortive effort. For instance, he sought liberalization, appointed to his staff economists identified with this position, put into cold storage the Council of Economic Advisers which had been identified with socialist sympathies, and then succumbed just a few months later to political pressures to revive the Council with economists who were still wedded to export pessimism and the older ways of planning *de facto* for stagnation. The resulting signals were those of ambivalence, furthering bureaucratic inaction out of prudence, and taking the steam out of the implementation of the attempted reforms. By contrast, the Prime Minister today has chosen and supports fully the reform-minded Finance Minister, had an excellent reform-minded Minister of State in charge of Commerce and Industry,[8] and the Finance Minister has chosen a team of economists to assist him that clearly shares his objectives, his plans, and his measures. The credibility of the reforms is correspondingly far greater. This credibility should permit and even prompt economic decisions by economic agents that would fulfil the expectations aroused by the reforms.

Moreover, the reforms are being unfolded in a

---

[7] Under Mrs Gandhi, the June 1966 devaluation and related policy changes, analysed extensively in J. Bhagwati and T. N. Srinivasan, *India* (New York: Columbia University Press, 1975), qualify as a liberalizing episode. The 1984 flurry of Committee work on liberalization does not: Mrs Gandhi's assassination prevented any follow-through under her watch, as already noted.

[8] He later resigned, following the financial scandal described below.

blitzkrieg of successive moves that both give them a momentum and keep opposition off balance. This strategy is reminiscent of the 'bicycle theory': just as you keep cycling so as not to fall off, you should keep going from reform to reform to prevent the opposition from concentrating forces at any static target of opportunity.[9] Thus, the reforms have moved over a number of areas, in rapid succession, and are now poised to enter new areas, admittedly of greater difficulty. I will describe them now, while drawing attention to the difficulties they face.

Controls

Recall that the control system was characterized by an interlocking and mutually reinforcing set of internal and external controls. To remove it, or to moderate its impact, it would not be enough to dismantle either the domestic licensing system or the exchange controls: both had to go. Of course, there had been a school of thought when Rajiv Gandhi was seen prematurely to be dismantling the system, that the sensible approach would be to sequence the reform such that domestic delicensing would precede the external liberalization via a return to current account convertibility. The idea was to get industry 'used' to competition internally, only then to expose it to the rigours of free external competition. This two-step sequencing is contrary, of course, to the everything-at-once, reforms-at-one-leap school of thought that Poland and Yeltsin's Russia have embraced. But the jury is still out in those countries as to whether you should cross a chasm in one leap or whether you should drop a bridge. In any event, a sequencing strategy may be hard

---

[9] The bicycle theory is used to justify multilateral trade negotiations: if you keep engaged in multilateral negotiations, you can ward off protectionists by claiming that you cannot oblige them as long as these negotiations are continuing. If you stop the multilateral negotiations, you succumb to protectionist demands: you fall off the bicycle.

to devise for countries which seek reforms from conditions of political and economic chaos, where Bakunin reigns more effectively than Adam Smith.

Regardless of the principles of ideal reform, the Rao government, faced with the foreign exchange crisis, had little alternative to adopting the sequencing route, with the dismantling of the domestic control machinery immediately attended to and the removal of exchange controls on current account only a stated objective, to be pursued more effectively later (as it was, in fact, later in the 1992 Budget).

Thus, the Finance Minister, who announced major reforms in his budget and in the Statement of Industrial Policy that he placed before the Lok Sabha (parliament) on 24 July 1991, boldly began with the task of domestic delicensing:[10]

• Industrial licensing was finally removed for new and old projects, whether for creation or expansion of capacity or for product diversification, except in eighteen industries and for locational reasons linked wholly to city planning and pollution management.[11]

• Barriers to entry in the shape of pre-entry clearance requirements imposed on 'large' or 'dominant' firms under the Monopolies and Restrictive Trade Practices Act were eliminated, to be replaced by regulation through policing of restrictive and unfair trade practices as with regulatory agencies elsewhere that attend to competition policy.

There was little dismantling of the controls at the level of the states. But, once the licensing machinery was dis-

---

[10] An excellent summary is provided in the internal documentation provided by the India Country Department of the World Bank, 23 Aug. 1991. I draw on this freely, though the essential facts are familiar from original sources in New Delhi.

[11] i.e. for projects to be located within 25 km of the 23 large cities with population of over 1 million, except in non-polluting industries or when the location was in designated industrial areas.

mantled by the centre, one could count on competition for investments (no longer allocated politically by the centre) among states to result in progressive freeing of the system from state-level controls.

Trade Regime

The reforms in regard to trade and exchange controls, however, were (for reasons just outlined) nowhere near so dramatic. The Rupee was devalued in July and this obviously should have eased the pressure on the foreign exchanges in tandem with the fiscal restraints announced in the budget.

There was a substantive replay of the 1966 episode of devaluation-cum-liberalization in that, along with the substantial devaluation, the export subsidies (the so-called Cash Compensatory Support) running at an average 6 per cent of the f.o.b. value of exports were eliminated. The exchange rate was to do the job of improving the effective exchange rate for exports, rather than export-subsidy schemes that encourage corruption of the Customs, put a burden on the exchequer, and are inevitably set in a manner that gives differential incentives to different exports on the basis of unjustified criteria.[12] Equally, the introduction of the Exim Scrip programme, under which 30 per cent of export earnings could be held for oneself and traded in a market where the exchange could be used freely for a large range of imports of intermediates and capital goods, thus introducing a substantial degree of flexibility and some space for covertibility, was a throwback to the Export Bonus Voucher schemes of the 1960s on the Indian subcontinent. Paul Rosenstein-Rodan, a

---

[12] The advantages of replacing export subsidies and import tariffs by a devaluation, even though they are often treated as 'equivalent', were discussed intensively at the time of the June 1966 devaluation. The concepts used to take into account the off-setting elimination of export subsidies and import tariffs when devaluing were 'gross' and 'net' devaluations. Cf. Bhagwati and Srinivasan, fn. 7, above.

Bloomsbury fan, used to say that promiscuity is easier than marriage; and flirting, however outrageously, with convertibility was easier than going all the way. Though, this time around, the intention was clearly to go on to tie the wedding bands: the Finance Minister had declared firmly that he planned within three years, should he survive, to eliminate licensing for most imports of capital goods and intermediates and to reach convertibility on the current account within three to five years.

In fact, by March 1992, this was already done with the move to what was christened 'partial' convertibility.[13] In essence, there was really full convertibility on current account whereas the epithet 'partial' referred to the fact that there were differential exchange rates facing exporters and importers.[14] More precisely, the exporters of goods and services surrendered their foreign earnings so as to get Rupees at a weighted exchange rate: 40 per cent at a lesser, official rate and 60 per cent at a better, market rate. As for imports, the 40 per cent exchange earnings were used to finance imports of 'essential commodities'—crude oil, diesel, kerosene, and fertilizers—on government account at the lesser official rate whereas private-sector imports were financed at the higher, market rate. In effect, therefore, there were three rates: one on exports and two on imports. The result, of course, was that governmental subsidization of essential imports was at the expense of exporters and, on private transactions, there was a bias against exports.

---

[13] This move was recommended by the High Level Committee on Balance of Payments headed by the former Deputy Governor of the Reserve Bank of India, Dr Rangarajan, whose Interim Report is published in the *Reserve Bank of India Bulletin* (Aug. 1992), 1293–304.

[14] Trade restrictions continued on consumer goods, while other imports were virtually on automatic licensing. Thus, current account convertibility was not as clear-cut and meaningful as one would like. But the move was a giant step forward. Tariffs also continue to play an important role in restricting and distorting trade, and need reform. But the role of customs duties in India's total tax revenue has grown instead of shrinking (as seen from Fig. A4 in the Statistical Appendix), and this complicates the task of reform.

Neither is a desirable state of affairs; and the relevant question now is the timing of the move to unification of the rates, or what is misleadingly called 'full' convertibility. With the differential between the black market and the free market rates now narrowed considerably, and foreign exchange reserves in better shape, this move may not be long delayed, barring unforeseen difficulties posed by phenomena such as a bad harvest or the collapse of the government.[15]

Direct Foreign Investment

The domestic delicensing was accompanied in July 1977 by a strictly limited but definite relaxation of earlier restrictions on investments by foreign firms. Thus, for example, automatic licensing was now to be given for projects involving foreign equity investment up to 51 per cent in 'high-priority' industries but only under conditions such as the self-financing of foreign exchange for capital goods imports and profit repatriation. But, down the road, additional changes were made to seduce multinationals into coming into India. A new foreign investment policy was promulgated in November 1991, easing the entry requirements further.

The emphasis has clearly shifted from the early almost-exclusive emphasis on arm's length technology transfers to cultivating direct equity investments. The message is sought to be conveyed in several ways to multinationals hitherto turned away and turned off by India's rejectionist attitudes and policies. A surefire sign was the visit by the Prime Minister himself to Davos, Switzerland, for the World Economic Forum meetings (in February 1992), which typically bring together the

[15] As this manuscript goes to press (Sept. 1992), the monsoon looks good and the minority Rao government appears to have shrewdly managed to obtain a majority in parliament through the break-up of the Janata Dal. In contrast to June 1966, when the harvest failed and Mrs Gandhi faced internal dissension and revolt, the situation now looks more optimistic.

CEOs of multinationals from the OECD countries, a clutch of prominent politicians and eminent academics from these countries, and the Prime Ministers of the developing countries that are shifting gear towards economic reform and seeking to get across the message of the new investor-friendly, open-door policy in their hitherto reluctant countries.

Public-Sector Enterprises

The final element of the constraining Indian policy framework that I addressed in Chapter 2 was the substantial presence of inefficient public enterprises. More than the reform of industrial and trade controls, and even the opening of India to foreign investment, the reform of public-sector enterprises runs into deeply held ideological beliefs. Their outright privatization is in consequence a political solution that the government has shied away from.

There are theories of second-best in economic science; and effective politics has to consist in the negotiation of one's reform agenda around minefields as best one can. Short of privatization, the government has undertaken to implement some changes that are satisfying, not maximizing, solutions. In particular, the scope of the public sector is to be more narrowly circumscribed than hitherto, and its exclusive domain is further to be confined to eight, rather than the earlier eighteen, areas: defence equipment, atomic energy, coal, petroleum, railways, and selected mining. Off the list are aircraft and airlines, shipbuilding, telecommunications equipment, electric power, iron and steel, heavy electrical equipment, and heavy castings and forgings.

But these policy changes and the announcement yet again of the conventional measures to finally improve the working of public enterprises through more autonomy and greater hiring of professionals do not add up to an effective attack on the problem posed by the public-sector enterprises. Only the imposition of hard budget constraints and the pressure of competition as it materializes thanks to the reforms I have described will produce the efficiency that has eluded them so far. In turn, the effective political imposition of hard budget constraints is likely to require the ability to shut down plants and to close firms, i.e. what is now called an 'exit policy'.

The government has come up with the idea of a National Renewal Fund, an odd description for an adjustment mechanism that would assist workers when laid off. It is not clear whether this will work in a country where turnover certainly exists in the unorganized private sector but is seriously constrained in the organized public sector. The public sector has manifestly operated so far on the assumption that, given the scarcity of jobs, it is bad enough to find one job in a lifetime and to ask people to find two is nothing short of cruel and unusual punishment. Without effective exit, the efficiency gains from other reforms will remain limited, for sure.

PROSPECTS OF SUCCESS

These are but the chief elements, still unfolding, of a substantial reform programme that resembles a clean-up operation after a visitation by a typhoon. The fiscal system, excessively dependent on indirect taxes and in turn on import duties, must also be reformed if the proposed reduction in tariffs in the interest of efficiency will reduce the already precarious revenues. Then again, financial-sector liberalization, essential to the successful functioning of industry, must also proceed apace.[16]

---

[16] I omitted this from the analysis in Ch. 2, but it is clearly important if the now liberated private sector is to function with maximum efficiency.

As the financial reforms are undertaken, with interest rates on term loans decontrolled and the private sector allowed to set up mutual funds, for example, the government faces the prospect of financial scandals, even when exogenous to its actions, undermining the credibility of the reforms: as the recent Indian Stock Market scandal almost did. The distinction between imprudent financial deregulation of the kind that led to the S & L crisis in the United States and the clearing up of the foolishly constraining regulatory debris on the Indian financial scene is too important to be blurred. But it certainly will be.

There are certain to be roadblocks as the reform process gathers momentum. I have already suggested several reasons why the reforms might hold this time, pointing to favourable factors that did not obtain in earlier episodes of attempted reform. But more can be said, and not all is so sanguine.

1. Nothing succeeds like success. If the microeconomic reforms could produce quick and substantial results, that would certainly help. But it is not clear that they would. The 1980s showed a significant improvement in the growth rate and it is tempting to attribute it to the limited reforms of Mrs Gandhi and then Rajiv Gandhi. Certainly, the improvement in the real exchange rate during this period improved export performance greatly and there is now substantial evidence that better exports and higher growth go together.

But the Latin-American style foreign borrowing that helped create the macroeconomic crisis was surely a major explanation of this prosperity as well, just as it created the debt-led growth of Latin America in the 1970s (only to be followed by the disastrous reversal in the 1980s). So too a role was played in the 1980s by the domestic budgetary spending that created jobs and the explosion of expenditure on wages and salaries: this created national income but is probably better seen as transfers, pointing to the well-known problem that in services the output is often measured by the input.

Perhaps the more dramatic and cascading reforms this time will produce quick and substantial gains in income. But remember also that the new need for stabilization, and the associated fiscal and monetary restraints, will offset the expansion that the microeconomic reforms could bring in the short run. Indeed, the reduced growth rate in 1991 only underlines this problem. So, there is cause for worry.

2. While the reality of the adverse effect of stabilization cannot be eliminated, the damage it does to the prospects of successful reform could be moderated. In particular, it is necessary to blunt the effect of the austerity programme, which should be felt mostly in the urban areas where labour is likely to be laid off as plants close due to lack of demand, by utilizing the Fair Price Shops to make fixed rations of food available to all at fixed prices (implying a dual-market solution, with prices and quantities freely traded in the private markets simultaneously).[17]

This would require getting food aid: this is not a problem today as both the EC and the United States are bending over backwards to find aid-financed markets for their agricultural production and have deliberately exempted the extension of market discipline via the Uruguay Round of GATT to such exports. Provided the terms of such aid are generous, and this could be the outcome of skilful negotiations that play off the EC against the United States, such food imports could play an important role in making India's transition to a more stable macroeconomic situation easier and therefore less likely to fail politically.

[17] The dual-market system has long been used in India to provide a minimum standard of living to the urban classes through the fixed rations at Fair Price Shops while leaving the open markets free so as to provide market incentives to farmers for more production. The economics of the dual-market is quite complex, of course, but its appeal is evident.

3. At the same time, just as Finance Minister V. P. Singh had utilized the income tax reform to generate visible success for the reform efforts when Rajiv Gandhi attempted his reforms, the Rao government can also profit from some visible signs of success in the short run. Will the influx of foreign investment increase dramatically enough to create this type of visible domestic confidence in the reforms? Since the change of policy announced on DFI some seven months ago, over a thousand foreign investment proposals involving a total investment of roughly half a billion US dollars have been approved, showing a sharp rise from the negligible levels earlier. But the sums are still small for a large country: they could grow substantially larger.

They should, if the advantages that India enjoys can be translated through policy into effective incentives. If the reforms are sustained, they will provide the best argument for the confidence that investors must enjoy before investments are made. The recent Mexican experience underlines this fact pretty well: the Mexican reforms have been sustained, unambiguous, and confidently explained and implemented, and the results in reversal of capital flight and influx of direct foreign investment are significant.

India, like China, which has also attracted massive foreign investment in recent years (even when netted out for investment by the overseas Chinese in Hong Kong and Taiwan), offers an immense market. But, domestic markets can only be part of the story: the big markets are international and the outward-oriented countries get the lion's share of investment over time.[18] India's effec-

---

[18] The thesis that inward-looking countries would not therefore be able to sustain large-scale inflows of foreign investment as well as the outward-oriented countries was advanced in my *Anatomy of Consequences of Exchange Control Regimes* (NBER, Cambridge, Mass.: Ballinger, 1978). Some econometric support for this thesis has been provided in V. N. Balasubramanyam and M. A. Salisu, 'Export Promotion, Import Substitution and Direct Foreign Investment in Less Developed Countries' in A. Koekkoek and L. B. M. Mennes (eds.), *International Trade and Global Development: Essays in Honour of Jagdish Bhagwati* (London: Routledge, 1991).

tive shift to outward-orientation, with the removal of anti-export bias entailed by the pre-reforms trade-and-payments regime, and the more investor-friendly policies towards foreign investors, should create the framework for a substantial and sustained inflow of investments.

India can also play a Japan card. Japanese aid and investments can be attracted both because there are no domestic difficulties in doing so and because Japan can be successfully lobbied to play such a role in India. There are two reasons why India faces less political difficulty in increasing the Japanese presence in her domestic economy. First, the Japanese did not manage to get to India in the Second World War, sparing India the atrocities that other Asian countries suffered in great measure. There are therefore no memories that make Japan's economic presence in India a political problem. Secondly, given the traditional worries about Western dominance, Japanese investments are likely to be seen as playing a useful countervailing or balancing role.

On the other hand, there are factors on the Japanese side that can be exploited to induce her to play a bigger role in India. Japanese foreign investments, now of great magnitude, have steadily moved westwards across from the Far Eastern super-performers—Taiwan, Singapore, and Hong Kong—to Malaysia, Indonesia, and Thailand, and (as wages in these countries also rise) are now generally considered to be poised to come to India. Again, Japan is increasingly likely to consider playing, both because of her own perceptions of her national interests and of her international role and because of demands from Asian countries, a major economic and developmental role in Asia, just as the United States is doing in South America and the European Community is doing in Eastern Europe. Thus, in response to the change in the United States' trade policy, with a trade bloc confined to the Americas (except for Israel) becoming her new policy objective, there are stirrings in Asia for a

Japan-centred 'defensive' trade bloc as well, with the initiative led by Malaysia.

While Japan may not respond to these demands, which are bound to grow, there is little doubt that she will see herself increasingly as playing a crucial Asian role in other ways. Instead of writing big cheques to finance tasks spelled out as of 'global' importance by the United States, tasks that surely reflect the latter's own economic and political interests, Japan is bound to move towards defining her own 'global' agenda, reflecting her own interests and perceptions. This is evident from the prominent role now being played by the UN High Commissioner for Refugees, Madame Sadako Ogata, giving Japan a leading voice in an issue that should, along with trade and the environment, dominate the 1990s. It is also manifest from Japan's energetic diplomatic and financial role at the Earth Summit in Rio in June 1992, when the United States was by contrast hesitant and uncertain. It is in fact hard to imagine Japan today acquiescing in the peculiar attribution of Japanese ideas and funds for debt relief to the US Treasury Secretary, Mr Nicholas Brady, as the 'Brady Plan', when in fact he and his predecessors had strenuously opposed proposals for debt relief earlier.

India, as a 'middle' Asian power, freed now from the baggage of friendship with the Soviet Union and hence suspicion from the Asian countries fearful of Soviet and communist threats to their international and domestic security, is now in a position to exploit diplomatically this new, if tentative, trend in Japan's foreign policy. In my judgement, the potential for mutual gain from such diplomatic initiatives is illustrated well by the opportunity missed by both the Asian developing countries and Japan during the Gulf crisis. While the United States pressured Japan into paying it grants worth nearly $US 13 billion for the Gulf War (money that could have been obtained instead from Saudi Arabia, Kuwait, and the

Emirates defended from Iraq), the five poor Asian countries (India, Bangladesh, Pakistan, Sri Lanka, and the
Philippines) that were adversely affected (each losing up
to $US 2–2.5 billion dollars annually), were left to fend
for themselves through loans from the multilateral institutions. Surely, it would have been more appropriate for
Japan to be using her funds to assist these poor and
hard-hit Asian countries instead. Aside from its greater
moral legitimacy (since aiding Bangladesh and India
makes more sense than aiding the United States, unless
one's moral sense is bizarre), the expenditure of these
funds in these Asian countries would have established
Japan as an economic superpower which took its responsibility in its own region quite seriously and exercised
foreign policy initiatives of its own choosing.

It remains to be seen whether a similar expropriation
of Japanese aid funds, away from the potential recipients
in Asia, towards the Commonwealth of Independent
States, will now occur again under pressure from the
cash-strapped United States, or whether Japan can be
persuaded to play an independent, and more appropriate
Asia-focused role in her future aid and investments.
Indian diplomacy needs to be harnessed towards this outcome, requiring that India begin to play an Asian role.

Finally, the reforms require that their rationale in the
context of India's afflictions and aspirations, and hence
their intellectual and political legitimacy, be clearly and
ceaselessly explained by the government. It is necessary
to argue forcefully that efficiency and growth are important, indeed given our immense poverty the most important, instruments for alleviating poverty. The reforms
under way are therefore part of the war against poverty,
not an agenda for growth in itself. This elementary, but
elemental, argument was never articulated by Rajiv
Gandhi who appeared, in consequence, to be pursuing
growth *per se*, reflecting a 'yuppie' fascination for technology, modernization, and growth as ends in themselves.

The new leadership is certainly aware that the chief virtue of our growth is that it will attack poverty directly by creating jobs and indirectly by raising the tax base to finance the programmes for aiding the poor. But it needs to develop the argument, using each opportunity to reiterate it, for otherwise the defunct economic doctrines will thrive again in the fields of neglect.

Equally, it is important to emphasize that the reforms are not a return to *laissez-faire*. They seek instead to move the government from counter-productive to productive intervention. There are plenty of things for the government to do, as both Indian intellectuals and masses appreciate and indeed Adam Smith himself recognized.[19] In fact, there is not the slightest danger of the present or any government deciding to self-destruct on anyone's prescribed schedule. But the failure to articulate this sentiment and to clarify this policy as 'liberal' reforms unfold is to invite for sure the obfuscating and damaging accusations of a return to *laissez-faire*.

CONCLUDING REMARK

The energy, talents, and worldly ambitions of India's many millions, captured so well in V. S. Naipaul's latest work that moves him from his earlier cynicism to great optimism,[20] need merely an appropriate policy framework to produce the economic magic that Jawaharlal Nehru wished for his compatriots but which, like many well-meaning intellectuals of his time, he mistakenly sought in now discredited economic doctrines. We finally have this elusive policy framework within our grasp.

[19] Few intellectuals are unaware, for example, of Adam Smith's well-known support of a governmental role in providing primary education to offset the deleterious effects of the division of labour on the labouring classes: cf. A. Smith, *The Wealth of Nations* (New York: Modern Library, 1937), 735-7.
[20] V. S. Naipaul, *India: A Million Mutinies Now* (London: Heinemann, 1990).

I must conclude with a story. An American trade negotiator, a friend of mine, went to India some years ago and met another friend, an ardent proponent of reforms, and said to him: 'You will be happy to know that Indians do very well in the United States, doing us also much good in consequence.' The quick-witted Indian, facing then an uphill task within the government in getting reforms going, replied: 'Ah, but make sure that you keep them out of your government.' My hope, and my expectation as well this time, is that this witticism will have soon yielded to successful change in India.

Statistical Appendix

This Appendix provides statistical information, in illustrated form, on key aspects of the Indian economy. The figures are referred to in the text at pages 18, 59, 64, and 88.

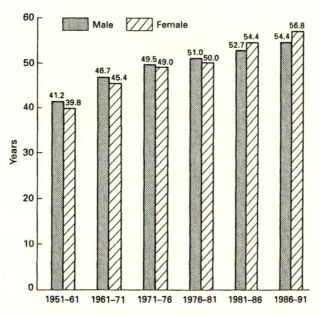

FIG. A1. Average life expectancy at birth in India, 1951–91
Note: 1981–6 and 1986–91 involve projections.
Source: The World Bank.

Statistical Appendix

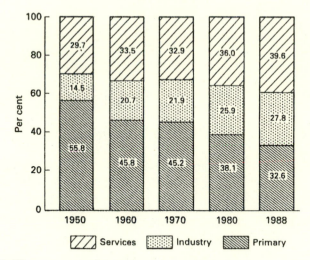

Fɪɢ. A2. The structure of GDP in India, 1980–1 prices (per cent)
Sources: National Account Statistics, Government of India;
V. Dubey, 'India: Economic Performance and Prospects', in E. Grilli
and D. Salvatore (eds.), *Handbook of Economic Development* (Oxford:
Pergamon Press, 1992).

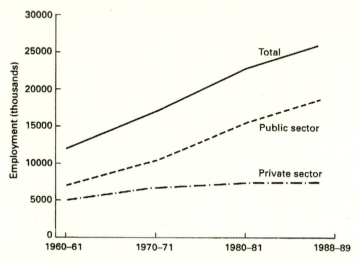

Fɪɢ. A3. Employment in the organized sector in India, 1960–89
*Provisional figures
Source: Economic Survey, Government of India.

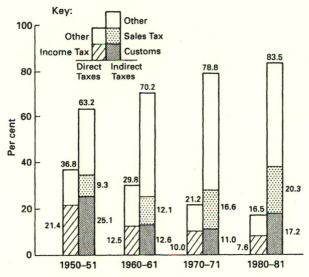

FIG. A4. The components of India's tax revenue (centre, states, and
union territories), 1950/1 to 1980/1
Sources: S. Acharya, 'India's Fiscal Policy', in R. E. B. Lucas and
G. Papanek (eds.), *The Indian Economy: Recent Development and
Future Prospects* (Boulder, Colo.: Westview Press, 1988), Table 14.10;
Dubey (see source for Table A1).

INDEX

Italic numbers denote reference to figures

accumulation 10, 11
Acharya, S. 103
Africa 19
agricultural sector 44, 89 n. 15
  growth 59
  and poverty 33–4
Ahluwalia, Isher J. 44, 45
Ahluwalia, Montek S. 34
Ahmed, Mahfooz 43
autarky 9, 35
authoritarianism 20–1
  see also totalitarianism

Balassa, Bela 45
Balasubramanyam, V. N. 94 n. 18
Balogh, Thomas 79
Bangladesh 12, 97
Barbados 28
Bardhan, Pranab 35
Bergson, Henri 46
Berliner, J. 62, n. 31
'bicycle' theory 85
Bofors scandal 81
'Bombay Plan' 29 n. 27
border war with China 7
borrowing, government 66, 68
  net public debt *67*
Brady, Nicholas 96
Brecher, R. 35 n. 39
'broad-banding' 50, 80, 81
Buiter, W. 67, 68 n. 37
bureaucracy 79
  see also control system; licensing

Cambodia 13
capital, gross domestic *41*
capital-intensive sectors 44
Cash Compensatory Support 87
Chakravarty, Professor Sukhamoy
  24 n. 22, 29 n. 27, 43 n. 5, 44,
  53, 59
children 47–9
China 6–7
  falls from favour 16–17

investment in 94
over-optimism inside 15
as rival to India 7–8, 10
USA and 6, 11–17
Chou En-lai 11
CIS (Commonwealth of Independent
  States) 76
  see also Gorbachev; Yeltsin
civil service 8, 72
coalition governments 72
Cohen, Morris 1
Cold War 6, 7
communism and communist states,
  see China; Marxism; USSR
compositional shift 44–6
Congress Party 8, 72
control system ('permit raj') 49–56,
  60, 61–2, 79
  reforms 85–7
  see also licensing
convertibility, current account 85,
  87, 88–9
corruption 53, 56, 81, 87, 92
credit rating 68, 75
crisis, macroeconomic 67–83
  see also reforms

Dahrendorf, R. 20 n. 14
delicensing 78, 80, 85, 86, 88, 89
democracy, Indian 8, 18, 19–20, 21
  economic strictures under 10–11
Deng Xiaoping 14, 15
Desai, Padma 13 n. 6, 42, 60 n. 28
devaluation 87
development, support for economic 9
DFI (Direct Foreign Investment)
  57–62, 75–6, 89–90, 94
Dobb, Maurice 10
Dubey, V. 102, 103

Earth Summit, Rio 96
Eastern Europe 7, 85
EC (European Community) 93, 95
education, primary 47, 49

enlightened self-interest 76–7
ethnic and religious problems 18–19
Etienne, Gilbert 31
Exim Scrip programme 87
'exit policies' 91
'export pessimism' 57
exports *58*, *59*, 88
    failure to develop 57–8, 61
    subsidies (Cash Compensatory
        Support) 87

Fabianism 21, 62–3, 78
Fair Price Shops 93
Far East:
    growth in 21, 24, 49
    see also Cambodia; China; Japan
        Malaysia; Philippines; Taiwan
far-sighted economists 68 n. 38
Felman–Mahalanobis model 53
Five-Year Plans 9, 22, 63
Fleming, Marcus 69 n. 39
food rationing 93
Friedman, Edward 12
Frisch, Ragnar 9

Galbraith, John Kenneth 7
Gandhi, Indira 14, 19, 73–4, 78, 84,
    89 n. 15, 92
Gandhi, Rajiv 14, 15 n. 9, 16, 73–4,
    75, 97
    reforms 78–80, 81–2, 84, 85, 92
GATT (General Agreement on
    Tariffs and Trade) 6, 93
GDP (Gross Domestic Product) *23*,
    33, *102*
Ghosh, Arun 24 n. 23
GNP (Gross National Product) 33
Gorbachev, Mikhail 77, 83
Green Revolution 44
growth 39, 40, 49, 71
    and attack on poverty 25–37
    distortion of 35–6
    rates of 22–5, 30, 39–40, 43, 92
    as 'rival' to poverty removal 27–31
    and savings 40
    strategy of rapid 30
    as 'trickle-down strategy' 31–2
    underestimated? 43
Gulf War 96–7
Gupta, S. P. 43

Harrison, Selig 18–19
Harrod–Domar model 10, 39–40, 52

Hatta, T. 35 n. 39
Hayek, F. von 51
Hirschman, A. 52
Hong Kong 94
Hook, Sidney 1

IMF (International Monetary Fund)
    6, 65, 68–9, 73
import substitution 55
imports 88
'incomes, minimum' 29–30
India:
    conspectus 17–18
    eclipsed in favour of China 11–13
    economic influence on 21
    economic model fails 17–18, 20
    goodwill towards 5–11, 14–16
    political success 18–22
    industrialization 58–61
    see also controls; licensing;
        technology
Industry Policy Resolutions 63
inefficient operation 60–1, 64–6
    see also corruption
inflation 72
international institutions 6
investment:
    allocation strategies 52–6
    direct foreign (DFI) 57–62, 75–6,
        89–90, 94
    productivity of 10–11

Jain, L. R. 34 n. 33
Janata Dal 74–5, 89 n. 15
Japan 23–4, 62
    economic influence of 21
    as potential investor 95–7
Joshi, Vijay 41, 66, 68 n. 37, 71

Kakwani, N. 35 n. 38
Kalecki, Michal 30
Kansal, S. M. 34 n. 33
Kennedy, John F. 7
Khatkhate, D. 71 n. 1
Kohli, Atul 10
Korea, *see* South Korea
Krishna, Raj 3
Krueger, Anne 3 n. 4, 61 n. 30
Kuwait crisis 68, 75, 96

laissez-faire 98
Lakdawala, D. T. 36 nn. 40–1
Lange–Lerner argument 51, 64–5

Latin America 24, 77, 92, 94
Laxman, R. K. 56
Lerner, *see* Lange–Lerner
Lewis, Arthur 79
Lewis, J. 7 n. 1
liberalization 73–4
  see also licensing, ended; privatization; reforms
licensing 50–1, 53, 55–6, 60
  ended 78, 80, 85, 86, 88, 89
life expectancy *101*
literacy 47, *48*, 49
Little, Ian M. D. 2 n. 3, 7, 57
  V. Joshi and 41, 66, 68 n. 37, 71
Lucas and Roemer models 25 n. 24

McFarlane, Bruce 12
Mahalanobis, Professor 9
  see also Felman–Mahalanobis
Malaysia 96
Malenbaum, Wilfred 7
Mao Tse-tung 15, 16, 28
market, trusting the 51
market-oriented reforms 16
Marxism 10, 63
Mathur, S. 34
Maxwell, Neville 12–13
Mazumdar, Dipak 54–5
microeconomics 54–5, 71–3, 92–3
Mill, James 2
Milliken, Max 7, 24 n. 22
Minhas, Bagicha S. 25 n. 25, 31,
  33–4, 34 n. 33
MIT Center for International Studies
  7
Monopolies and Restrictive Trade
  Practices (MRTP) 80–1, 86
Moore, Barrington 19–20
Morgenbesser, Sidney 28
MRTP, *see* Monopolies
multinationals 89–90
Mundell, Robert 69 n. 39
Murphy, K. M. 53
Myrdal, Gunnar 72

Naipaul, V. S. 98
National Front government 74
National Renewal Fund 91
Nayyar, B. R. 64 n. 33
Nehru, Jawaharlal 6, 8, 9–10, 62, 98
Nixon, Richard M. 7, 11, 76
NRIs (non-resident Indians) 75
Nurkse, Ragnar 57

Ogata, Madame Sadako 96
oil:
  crises 45–6, 67
  surcharge 74
  organized sector, employment *102*
  outward-orientation 95

Pakistan 11–12, 19, 97
Panagariya, A. 61 n. 29
Pant, Pitambar 9, 29
parallel economy 43
Patel, I. G. 82
Patel, U. 67, 68 n. 37
'permit raj', *see* control system
Philippines 97
Planning Commission 29
Polak, Jacques 69 n. 39
Poland 85
policy framework 46–7
poverty:
  attack on 8–9, 25–37, 60–1
  and democracy 19–20
Prebisch, Raul 57
prices, consumer *73*
privatization, in public sector 90
productivity 40
  why low? 46–9
  see also growth
Protestantism 49
public sector 62–6, 71
  profitability 65–6
  reforms 90–1
  scope 90
  size 63–4
'pull-up' 32, 34, 71
  see also 'trickle-down'
Pye, Lucien 12

Radhakrishnan, Sarvapalli 1
Raj, Professor K. N. 24 n. 22, 42–3,
  45, 59, 60 n. 26
Rangarajan, Dr 88 n. 13
Rao, Narasimha, government. 74
  see also reforms
Ravallion, M. 25 n. 25
Raychaudhuri, T. 29 n. 27'
Reagan administration 14–15
Reddaway, Brian 7
redistribution 26
reforms, Rajiv Gandhi government
  78–80, 81–2, 84, 85, 92
reforms, Rao government 16, 69, 82,
  84–99,

reforms, Rao government (*cont.*):
  controls 85–7
  direct foreign investment 89–90
  fiscal 91
  prospects of success 91–9
  public sector 91–1
  scene set for 83
  trade 87–9
regional policies 56
rentier economy 60
restraints, *see* control system
Richman, Barry 13
Robinson, Joan 28
Roemer, *see* Lucas
Rosen, George 7
Rosenstein-Rodan, Paul H. 7, 52, 87–8
Rostow, Walt 7
Russell, Bertrand 1
Russia, *see* CIS; USSR

Saith, A. 34
Salisu, M. A. 94 n. 18
Saluja, M. R. 34 n. 33
savings 21, 30, 40–1, *66*, 66
  overestimated? 42–3
  see also growth
Schleifer, A. 53
Scitovsky, Tibor 2 n. 3
Scott, Maurice 2 n. 3
Second World War, recovery from 6
self-reliance models 12–13
'sequencing' route to reform 85, 86
'Shanghai Communique' 11
'sick units' 64 n. 35, 65
Singh, Dr Manmohan (Rao's
  Finance Minister) 3, 16, 57, 83, 86, 88
Singh, V. P. 79, 81–2, 94
small-scale sector, protecting 54–5
Smith, Adam 1, 98
South Korea 23, 33, 46, 58, 59, 62
Soviet Union, *see* USSR
Spencer, Herbert 60
spending, government 66, 67
  see also public sector
Sri Lanka 97
Srinivasan, T. N. 29 n. 27, 31, 34, 35, 43, 44–5, 60 n. 26
  J. Bhagwati and 3, 43 n. 6, 44–5, 84

stabilization, dangers 93
state-level reforms 86–7
Statistical Institute 29
structural reforms 68–9
Subbarao, K. 25 n. 25, 35 n. 38, 36

Taiwan 23, 33, 94
tariffs 88 n. 14, 91
  GATT 6, 93
tax revenue *103*
  and GDP 21–2
technology, and investment 61–2
Tendulkar, S. 25 n. 25
textile industry 54–5
Thakurdas, P., *et al.* 29 n. 27
theory, economic 46
think-tanks 29
Tinbergen, Jan 9
totalitarianism 6–7, 10
trade:
  foreign 57–61, 87–9
  policies, *see also* bureaucracy;
    control system; industrialization;
    licensing
  'trickle-down' 31–2, 34

USA (United States):
  1950s 5–6
  agricultural production 93
  and China 6, 11–17
  domestic spending 77
  and India 15
  and Latin America 95
  see also Cold War
USSR (Soviet Union) 6–7, 11, 61, 76, 77
  end of 76
  growth and savings rates 40, *42*
  and India 12, 14, 96
  see also CIS; Cold War

Varshney, A. 20 n. 15

Weiner, Myron 33 n. 31, 47–9
Weisskopf, Thomas 13
Wolf, M. 57 n. 23
World Bank 6, 14–15, 23, 45, 68–9, 86 n. 10, 101

Yeltsin, Boris 77, 85

Printed in the United States
35874LVS00001B/103-123